SHAKUNTALA

AND OTHER WRITINGS

By

KALIDASA

Translated with an introduction by

ARTHUR W. RYDER

Preface by

G. L. ANDERSON

A Dutton dep *Paperback*

NEW YORK
E. P. DUTTON & CO., INC.

This paperback edition of
"SHAKUNTALA AND OTHER WRITINGS"
Published 1959 by E. P. Dutton & Co., Inc.

CONTENTS

INTRODUCTION

KALIDASA—HIS LIFE AND WRITINGS

I

KALIDASA probably lived in the fifth century of the Christian era. This date, approximate as it is, must yet be given with considerable hesitation, and is by no means certain. No truly biographical data are preserved about the author, who nevertheless enjoyed a great popularity during his life, and whom the Hindus have ever regarded as the greatest of Sanskrit poets. We are thus confronted with one of the remarkable problems of literary history. For our ignorance is not due to neglect of Kalidasa's writings on the part of his countrymen, but to their strange blindness in regard to the interest and importance of historic fact. No European nation can compare with India in critical devotion to its own literature. During a period to be reckoned not by centuries but by millenniums, there has been in India an unbroken line of savants unselfishly dedicated to the perpetuation and exegesis of the native masterpieces. Editions, recensions, commentaries abound; poets have sought the exact phrase of appreciation for their predecessors: yet when we seek to reconstruct the life of their greatest poet, we have no materials except certain tantalising legends, and such data as we can gather from the writings of a man who hardly mentions himself.

One of these legends deserves to be recounted for its intrinsic interest, although it contains, so far as we can see, no grain of historic truth, and although it places Kalidasa in Benares, five hundred miles distant from the only city in which we certainly know that he spent a part of his life. According to this account, Kalidasa was a Brahman's child. At the age of six months he was left an orphan and was adopted by an ox-driver. He grew to manhood without formal education, yet with remarkable beauty and grace of manner. Now it happened that the Princess of Benares was a blue-stocking, who rejected one suitor after another, among them her father's counsellor, because they failed to reach her standard as scholars and poets. The rejected counsellor planned a cruel revenge. He took the handsome ox-driver from the street, gave him the garments of a savant and a retinue of learned doctors, then introduced him to the princess, after warning him that he was under no circumstances to open his lips. The princess was struck with his beauty and smitten to the depths of her pedantic soul by his obstinate silence, which seemed to her, as indeed it was, an evidence of profound wisdom. She desired to marry Kalidasa, and together they went to the temple. But no sooner was the ceremony performed than Kalidasa perceived an image of a bull. His early training was too much for him; the secret came out, and the bride was furious. But she relented in response to Kalidasa's entreaties, and advised him to pray for learning and poetry to the goddess Kali. The prayer was granted; education and poetical power descended miraculously to dwell with the young ox-driver, who in gratitude assumed the name Kalidasa, servant of Kali. Feeling that he owed this happy change in his very nature to his princess, he swore that he would ever treat her as his teacher, with profound respect but without familiarity. This was more than the lady had bargained for; her anger burst forth anew, and she cursed Kalidasa to meet his death at the hands of a woman. At a later date, the story continues, this curse was fulfilled. A certain king had written a half-stanza of verse, and had offered a large reward to any poet who could worthily complete it. Kalidasa completed the stanza without difficulty; but a woman whom he loved discovered his lines, and greedy of the reward herself, killed him.

Another legend represents Kalidasa as engaging in a pilgrimage to a shrine of Vishnu in Southern India, in company with two other famous writers, Bhavabhuti and Dandin. Yet another pictures Bhavabhuti as a contemporary of Kalidasa, and jealous of the less austere poet's reputation. These stories must be untrue, for it is certain that the three authors were not contemporary, yet they show a true instinct in the belief that genius seeks genius, and is rarely isolated.

This instinctive belief has been at work with the stories which connect Kalidasa with King Vikramaditya and the literary figures of his court. It has doubtless enlarged, perhaps partly falsified the facts; yet we cannot doubt that there is truth in this tradition, late though it be, and impossible though it may ever be to separate the actual from the fanciful. Here then we are on firmer ground.

King Vikramaditya ruled in the city of Ujjain, in West-central India. He was mighty both in war and in peace, winning especial glory by a decisive victory over the barbarians who pressed into India through the northern passes. Though it has not proved possible to identify this monarch with any of the known rulers, there can be no doubt that he existed and had the character attributed to him. The name Vikramaditya—Sun of Valour—is probably not a proper name, but a title like Pharaoh or Tsar. No doubt Kalidasa intended to pay a tribute to his patron, the Sun of Valour, in the very title of his play, *Urvashi won by Valour*.

King Vikramaditya was a great patron of learning and of poetry. Ujjain during his reign was the most brilliant capital in the world, nor has it to this day lost all the lustre shed upon it by that splendid court. Among the eminent men gathered there, nine were particularly distinguished, and these nine are known as the "nine gems." Some of the nine gems were poets, others represented science—astronomy, medicine, lexicography. It is quite true that the details of this late tradition concerning the nine gems are open to suspicion, yet the central fact is not doubtful: that there was at this time and place a great quickening of the human mind, an artistic impulse creating works that cannot perish. Ujjain in the days of Vikramaditya stands worthily beside Athens, Rome, Florence, and London in their great centuries. Here is the substantial fact behind Max Müller's often ridiculed theory of the renaissance of Sanskrit literature. It is quite false to suppose, as some appear to do, that this theory has been invalidated by the discovery of certain literary products which antedate Kalidasa. It might even be said that those rare and happy centuries that see a man as great as Homer or Vergil or Kalidasa or Shakespeare partake in that one man of a renaissance.

It is interesting to observe that the centuries of intellectual darkness in Europe have sometimes coincided with centuries of light in India. The Vedas were composed for the most part before Homer; Kalidasa and his contemporaries lived while Rome was tottering under barbarian assault.

To the scanty and uncertain data of late traditions may be added some information about Kalidasa's life gathered from his own writings. He mentions his own name only in the prologues to his three plays, and here with a modesty that is charming indeed, yet tantalising. One wishes for a portion of the communicativeness that characterises some of the Indian poets. He speaks in the first person only once, in the verses introductory to his epic poem *The Dynasty of Raghu.*[1] Here also we feel his modesty, and here once more we are balked of details as to his life.

We know from Kalidasa's writings that he spent at least a part of his life in the city of Ujjain. He refers to Ujjain more than once, and in a manner hardly possible to one who did not know and love the city. Especially in his poem *The Cloud-Messenger* does he dwell upon the city's charms, and even bids the cloud make a détour in his long journey lest he should miss making its acquaintance.[2]

We learn further that Kalidasa travelled widely in India. The fourth canto of *The Dynasty of Raghu* describes a tour about the whole of India and even into regions which are beyond the borders of a narrowly measured India. It is hard to believe that Kalidasa had not himself made such a "grand tour"; so much of truth there may be in the tradition which sends him on a pilgrimage to Southern India. The thirteenth canto of the same epic and *The Cloud-Messenger* also describe long journeys over India, for the most part through regions far from Ujjain. It is the mountains which impress him most deeply. His works are full of the Himalayas. Apart from his earliest

[1] These verses are translated on pp. 123, 124.
[2] The passage will be found on pp. 190-192.

drama and the slight poem called *The Seasons*, there is not one of them which is not fairly redolent of mountains. One, *The Birth of the War-god*, might be said to be all mountains. Nor was it only Himalayan grandeur and sublimity which attracted him; for, as a Hindu critic has acutely observed, he is the only Sanskrit poet who has described a certain flower that grows in Kashmir. The sea interested him less. To him, as to most Hindus, the ocean was a beautiful, terrible barrier, not a highway to adventure. The "sea-belted earth" of which Kalidasa speaks means to him the mainland of India.

Another conclusion that may be certainly drawn from Kalidasa's writing is this, that he was a man of sound and rather extensive education. He was not indeed a prodigy of learning, like Bhavabhuti in his own country or Milton in England, yet no man could write as he did without hard and intelligent study. To begin with, he had a minutely accurate knowledge of the Sanskrit language, at a time when Sanskrit was to some extent an artificial tongue. Somewhat too much stress is often laid upon this point, as if the writers of the classical period in India were composing in a foreign language. Every writer, especially every poet, composing in any language, writes in what may be called a strange idiom; that is, he does not write as he talks. Yet it is true that the gap between written language and vernacular was wider in Kalidasa's day than it has often been. The Hindus themselves regard twelve years' study as requisite for the mastery of the "chief of all sciences, the science of grammar." That Kalidasa had mastered this science his works bear abundant witness.

He likewise mastered the works on rhetoric and dramatic theory—subjects which Hindu savants have treated with great, if sometimes hair-splitting, ingenuity. The profound and subtle systems of philosophy were also possessed by Kalidasa, and he had some knowledge of astronomy and law.

But it was not only in written books that Kalidasa was deeply read. Rarely has a man walked our earth who observed the phenomena of living nature as accurately as he, though his accuracy was of course that of the poet, not that of the scientist. Much is lost to us who grow up among other animals and plants; yet we can appreciate his "bee-black hair," his ashoka-tree that "sheds his blossoms in a rain of tears," his river wearing a sombre veil of mist:

> Although her reeds seem hands that clutch the dress
> To hide her charms;

his picture of the day-blooming water-lily at sunset:

> The water-lily closes, but
> With wonderful reluctancy;
> As if it troubled her to shut
> Her door of welcome to the bee.

The religion of any great poet is always a matter of interest, especially the religion of a Hindu poet; for the Hindus have ever been a deeply and creatively religious people. So far as we can judge, Kalidasa moved among the jarring sects with sympathy for all, fanaticism for none. The dedicatory prayers that introduce his dramas are addressed to Shiva. This is hardly more than a convention, for Shiva is the patron of literature. If one of his epics, *The Birth of the War-god*, is distinctively Shivaistic, the other, *The Dynasty of Raghu*, is no less Vishnuite in tendency. If the hymn to Vishnu in *The Dynasty of Raghu* is an expression of Vedantic monism, the hymn to Brahma in *The Birth of the War-god* gives equally clear expression to the rival dualism of the Sankhya system. Nor are the Yoga doctrine and Buddhism left without sympathetic mention. We are therefore justified in concluding that Kalidasa was, in matters of religion, what William James would call "healthy-minded," emphatically not a "sick soul."

There are certain other impressions of Kalidasa's life and personality which gradually become convictions in the mind of one who reads and re-reads his poetry, though they are less easily susceptible of exact proof. One feels certain that he was physically handsome, and the handsome Hindu is a wonderfully fine type of manhood. One knows that he possessed a fascination for women, as they in turn fascinated him. One knows that children loved him. One becomes convinced that he never suffered any morbid, soul-shaking experience such as besetting religious doubt brings with it, or the pangs of despised love; that on the contrary he moved among men and women with a serene and godlike tread, neither self-indulgent nor ascetic, with mind and senses ever alert to every form of beauty. We know that his poetry was popular while he lived, and we cannot doubt that his personality was equally attractive, though it is probable that no contemporary knew the full measure of his greatness. For his nature was one of singular balance, equally at home in a splendid court and on a lonely mountain, with men of high and of low degree. Such men are never fully appreciated during life. They continue to grow after they are dead.

II

Kalidasa left seven works which have come down to us: three dramas, two epics, one elegiac poem, and one descriptive poem. Many other works, including even an astronomical treatise, have been attributed to him; they are certainly not his. Perhaps there was more than one author who bore the name Kalidasa; perhaps certain later writers were more concerned for their work than for personal fame. On the other hand, there is no reason to doubt that the seven recognised works are in truth from Kalidasa's hand. The only one concerning which there is reasonable room for suspicion is the short poem descriptive of the seasons, and this is fortunately the least important of the seven. Nor is there evidence to show that any considerable poem has been lost, unless it be true that the concluding cantos of one of the epics have perished. We are thus in a fortunate position in reading Kalidasa: we have substantially all that he wrote, and run no risk of ascribing to him any considerable work from another hand.

Of these seven works, four are poetry throughout; the three dramas, like all Sanskrit dramas, are written in prose, with a generous mingling of lyric and descriptive stanzas. The poetry, even in the epics, is stanzaic; no part of it can fairly be compared to English blank verse. Classical Sanskrit verse, so far as structure is concerned, has much in common with familiar Greek and Latin forms:

it makes no systematic use of rhyme; it depends for its rhythm not upon accent, but upon quantity. The natural medium of translation into English seems to me to be the rhymed stanza; [1] in the present work the rhymed stanza has been used, with a consistency perhaps too rigid, wherever the original is in verse.

Kalidasa's three dramas bear the names: *Malavika and Agnimitra*, *Urvashi*, and *Shakuntala*. The two epics are *The Dynasty of Raghu* and *The Birth of the War-god*. The elegiac poem is called *The Cloud-Messenger*, and the descriptive poem is entitled *The Seasons*. It may be well to state briefly the more salient features of the Sanskrit *genres* to which these works belong.

The drama proved in India, as in other countries, a congenial form to many of the most eminent poets. The Indian drama has a marked individuality, but stands nearer to the modern European theatre than to that of ancient Greece; for the plays, with a very few exceptions, have no religious significance, and deal with love between man and woman. Although tragic elements may be present, a tragic ending is forbidden. Indeed, nothing regarded as disagreeable, such as fighting or even kissing, is permitted on the stage; here Europe may perhaps learn a lesson in taste. Stage properties were few and simple, while particular care was lavished on the music. The female parts were played by women. The plays very rarely have long monologues, even the inevitable prologue being divided between two speakers, but a Hindu audience was tolerant of lyrical digression.

It may be said, though the statement needs qualification in both directions, that the Indian dramas have less action and less individuality in the characters, but more poetical charm than the dramas of modern Europe.

On the whole, Kalidasa was remarkably faithful to the ingenious but somewhat over-elaborate conventions of Indian dramaturgy. His first play, the *Malavika and Agnimitra*, is entirely conventional in plot. The *Shakuntala* is transfigured by the character of the heroine. The *Urvashi*, in spite of detail beauty, marks a distinct decline.

[1] This matter is more fully discussed in the introduction to my translation of *The Little Clay Cart* (1905).

The Dynasty of Raghu and *The Birth of the War-god* belong to a species of composition which it is not easy to name accurately. The Hindu name *kavya* has been rendered by artificial epic, *épopée savante, Kunstgedicht.* It is best perhaps to use the term epic, and to qualify the term by explanation.

The *kavyas* differ widely from the *Mahabharata* and the *Ramayana,* epics which resemble the *Iliad* and *Odyssey* less in outward form than in their character as truly national poems. The *kavya* is a narrative poem written in a sophisticated age by a learned poet, who possesses all the resources of an elaborate rhetoric and metric. The subject is drawn from time-honoured mythology. The poem is divided into cantos, written not in blank verse but in stanzas. Several stanza-forms are commonly employed in the same poem, though not in the same canto, except that the concluding verses of a canto are not infrequently written in a metre of more compass than the remainder.

I have called *The Cloud-Messenger* an elegiac poem, though it would not perhaps meet the test of a rigid definition. The Hindus class it with *The Dynasty of Raghu* and *The Birth of the War-god* as a *kavya,* but this classification simply evidences their embarrassment. In fact, Kalidasa created in *The Cloud-Messenger* a new *genre.* No further explanation is needed here, as the entire poem is translated below.

The short descriptive poem called *The Seasons* has abundant analogues in other literatures, and requires no comment.

It is not possible to fix the chronology of Kalidasa's writings, yet we are not wholly in the dark. *Malavika and Agnimitra* was certainly his first drama, almost certainly his first work. It is a reasonable conjecture, though nothing more, that Urvashi was written late, when the poet's powers were waning. The introductory stanzas of *The Dynasty of Raghu* suggest that this epic was written before *The Birth of the War-god,* though the inference is far from certain. Again, it is reasonable to assume that the great works on which Kalidasa's fame chiefly rests—*Shakuntala, The Cloud-Messenger, The Dynasty of Raghu,* the first eight cantos of *The Birth of the War-god*—were composed when he was in the prime of manhood. But as to the succession of these four works we can do little but guess.

Kalidasa's glory depends primarily upon the quality of his work, yet would be much diminished if he had failed in bulk and variety. In India, more than would be the case in Europe, the extent of his writing is an indication of originality and power; for the poets of the classical period underwent an education that encouraged an exaggerated fastidiousness, and they wrote for a public meticulously critical. Thus the great Bhavabhuti spent his life in constructing three dramas; mighty spirit though he was, he yet suffers from the very scrupulosity of his labour. In this matter, as in others, Kalidasa preserves his intellectual balance and his spiritual initiative: what greatness of soul is required for this, every one knows who has ever had the misfortune to differ in opinion from an intellectual clique.

III

Le nom de Kâlidâsa domine la poésie indienne et la résume brillamment. Le drame, l'épopée savante, l'élégie attestent aujourd'hui encore la puissance et la souplesse de ce magnifique génie; seul entre les disciples de Sarasvatî [the goddess of eloquence], il a eu le bonheur de produire un chef-d'œuvre vraiment classique, où l'Inde s'admire et où l'humanité se reconnaît. Les applaudissements qui saluèrent la naissance de Çakuntalâ à Ujjayinî ont après de longs siècles éclaté d'un bout du monde à l'autre, quand William Jones l'eut révélée à l'Occident. Kâlidâsa a marqué sa place dans cette pléiade étincelante où chaque nom résume une période de l'esprit humain. La série de ces noms forme l'histoire, ou plutôt elle est l'histoire même.[1]

It is hardly possible to say anything true about Kalidasa's achievement which is not already contained in this appreciation. Yet one loves to expand the praise, even though realising that the critic is by his very nature a fool. Here

[1] Lévi, *Le Théâtre Indien*, p. 163.

there shall at any rate be none of that cold-blooded criticism which imagines itself set above a world-author to appraise and judge, but a generous tribute of affectionate admiration.

The best proof of a poet's greatness is the inability of men to live without him; in other words, his power to win and hold through centuries the love and admiration of his own people, especially when that people has shown itself capable of high intellectual and spiritual achievement.

For something like fifteen hundred years, Kalidasa has been more widely read in India than any other author who wrote in Sanskrit. There have also been many attempts to express in words the secret of his abiding power: such attempts can never be wholly successful, yet they are not without considerable interest. Thus Bana, a celebrated novelist of the seventh century, has the following lines in some stanzas of poetical criticism which he prefixes to a historical romance:

> Where find a soul that does not thrill
>   In Kalidasa's verse to meet
> The smooth, inevitable lines
>   Like blossom-clusters, honey-sweet?

A later writer, speaking of Kalidasa and another poet, is more laconic in this alliterative line: *Bhaso hasah, Kalidaso vilasah*—Bhasa is mirth, Kalidasa is grace.

These two critics see Kalidasa's grace, his sweetness, his delicate taste, without doing justice to the massive quality without which his poetry could not have survived.

Though Kalidasa has not been as widely appreciated in Europe as he deserves, he is the only Sanskrit poet who can properly be said to have been appreciated at all. Here he must struggle with the truly Himalayan barrier of language. Since there will never be many Europeans, even among the cultivated, who will find it possible to study the intricate Sanskrit language, there remains only one means of presentation. None knows the cruel inadequacy of poetical translation like the translator. He understands better than others can, the significance of the position which Kalidasa has won in Europe. When Sir William Jones first translated the *Shakuntala* in 1789, his work was enthusiastically received in Europe, and most warmly, as was fitting, by the greatest living poet of

Europe. Since that day, as is testified by new translations and by reprints of the old, there have been many thousands who have read at least one of Kalidasa's works; other thousands have seen it on the stage in Europe and America.

How explain a reputation that maintains itself indefinitely and that conquers a new continent after a lapse of thirteen hundred years? None can explain it, yet certain contributory causes can be named.

No other poet in any land has sung of happy love between man and woman as Kalidasa sang. Every one of his works is a love-poem, however much more it may be. Yet the theme is so infinitely varied that the reader never wearies. If one were to doubt from a study of European literature, comparing the ancient classics with modern works, whether romantic love be the expression of a natural instinct, be not rather a morbid survival of decaying chivalry, he has only to turn to India's independently growing literature to find the question settled. Kalidasa's love-poetry rings as true in our ears as it did in his countrymen's ears fifteen hundred years ago.

It is of love eventually happy, though often struggling for a time against external obstacles, that Kalidasa writes. There is nowhere in his works a trace of that not quite healthy feeling that sometimes assumes the name "modern love." If it were not so, his poetry could hardly have survived; for happy love, blessed with children, is surely the more fundamental thing. In his drama *Urvashi* he is ready to change and greatly injure a tragic story, given him by long tradition, in order that a loving pair may not be permanently separated. One apparent exception there is—the story of Rama and Sita in *The Dynasty of Raghu*. In this case it must be remembered that Rama is an incarnation of Vishnu, and the story of a mighty god incarnate is not to be lightly tampered with.

It is perhaps an inevitable consequence of Kalidasa's subject that his women appeal more strongly to a modern reader than his men. The man is the more variable phenomenon, and though manly virtues are the same in all countries and centuries, the emphasis has been variously laid. But the true woman seems timeless, universal. I know of no poet, unless it be Shakespeare, who has given the world a group of heroines so individual yet so universal; heroines as true, as tender, as brave as are Indumati, Sita, Parvati, the Yaksha's bride, and Shakuntala.

Kalidasa could not understand women without understanding children. It would be difficult to find anywhere lovelier pictures of childhood than those in which our poet presents the little Bharata, Ayus, Raghu, Kumara. It is a fact worth noticing that Kalidasa's children are all boys. Beautiful as his women are, he never does more than glance at a little girl.

Another pervading note of Kalidasa's writing is his love of external nature. No doubt it is easier for a Hindu, with his almost instinctive belief in reincarnation, to feel that all life, from plant to god, is truly one; yet none, even among the Hindus, has expressed this feeling with such convincing beauty as has Kalidasa. It is hardly true to say that he personifies rivers and mountains and trees; to him they have a conscious individuality as truly and as certainly as animals or men or gods. Fully to appreciate Kalidasa's poetry one must have spent some weeks at least among wild mountains and forests untouched by man; there the conviction grows that trees and flowers are indeed individuals, fully conscious of a personal life and happy in that life. The return to urban surroundings makes the vision fade; yet the memory remains, like a great love or a glimpse of mystic insight, as an intuitive conviction of a higher truth.

Kalidasa's knowledge of nature is not only sympathetic, it is also minutely accurate. Not only are the snows and windy music of the Himalayas, the mighty current of the sacred Ganges, his possession; his too are smaller streams and trees and every littlest flower. It is delightful to imagine a meeting between Kalidasa and Darwin. They would have understood each other perfectly; for in each the same kind of imagination worked with the same wealth of observed fact.

I have already hinted at the wonderful balance in Kalidasa's character, by virtue of which he found himself equally at home in a palace and in a wilderness. I know not with whom to compare him in this; even Shakespeare, for all his magical insight into natural beauty, is primarily a poet of the human heart. That can hardly be said of Kalidasa, nor can it be said that he is primarily a poet of natural beauty. The two characters unite in him, it might almost be said, chemically. The matter which I am clumsily endeavouring to make plain is beautifully epitomised in *The Cloud-Messenger*. The former half is a description of external nature, yet interwoven with human feeling; the latter half is a picture of a human heart, yet the picture is framed in natural beauty. So exquisitely is the thing done that none can say which half is superior. Of those who read this perfect poem in the original text, some are more moved by the one, some by the other. Kalidasa understood in the fifth century what Europe did not learn until the nineteenth, and even now comprehends only imperfectly: that the world was not made for man, that man reaches his full stature only as he realises the dignity and worth of life that is not human.

That Kalidasa seized this truth is a magnificent tribute to his intellectual power, a quality quite as necessary to great poetry as perfection of form. Poetical fluency is not rare; intellectual grasp is not very uncommon: but the combination has not been found perhaps more than a dozen times since the world began. Because he possessed this harmonious combination, Kalidasa ranks not with Anacreon and Horace and Shelley, but with Sophocles, Vergil, Milton.

He would doubtless have been somewhat bewildered by Wordsworth's gospel of nature. "The world is too much with us," we can fancy him repeating. "How can the world, the beautiful human world, be too much with us? How can sympathy with one form of life do other than vivify our sympathy with other forms of life?"

It remains to say what can be said in a foreign language of Kalidasa's style. We have seen that he had a formal and systematic education; in this respect he is rather to be compared with Milton and Tennyson than with Shakespeare or Burns. He was completely master of his learning. In an age and a country which reprobated carelessness but were tolerant of pedantry, he held the scales with a wonderfully even hand, never heedless and never indulging in the elaborate trifling with Sanskrit diction which repels the reader from much of Indian literature. It is true that some western critics have spoken of his disfiguring conceits and puerile plays on words. One can only wonder whether these critics have ever read Elizabethan literature; for Kalidasa's style is far less obnoxious to such condemnation than Shakespeare's. That he had a rich and glowing imagination, "excelling in metaphor," as the Hindus themselves affirm, is indeed true; that he may, both in youth and age, have written lines which would not have passed his scrutiny in the vigour of manhood, it is not worth while to deny: yet the total effect left by his poetry is one of extraordinary sureness and delicacy of taste. This is scarcely a matter for argument; a reader can do no more than state his own subjective impression, though he is glad to find that impression confirmed by the unanimous authority of fifty generations of Hindus, surely the most competent judges on such a point.

Analysis of Kalidasa's writings might easily be continued, but analysis can never explain life. The only real criticism is subjective. We know that Kalidasa is a very great poet, because the world has not been able to leave him alone.

ARTHUR W. RYDER

BERKELEY, CALIFORNIA
1912

PREFACE

The literary achievement of Kalidasa has long impressed Westerners. Goethe's interest in the *Shakuntala* and the elegant English translation of Sir William Jones (1789) brought the lyrical charm of Kalidasa's greatest work to appreciative European readers and called attention to his other plays and his poetry. But inevitably Kalidasa's literary efforts were judged by the standards of Western literary taste. The tradition of Western drama brings every playwright before the bar of Aristotle's *Poetics* and the achievement of Greek drama, and then to a more cosmopolitan court of appeal in the form of comparisons with the dramas of Shakespeare and of European Neo-Classicism. In this competition Kalidasa's plays are relegated to a sub-class of "lyrical dramas" and are comparable to Shakespeare's *As You Like It* or *The Tempest* rather than to *Lear, Hamlet* or *Othello*. This kind of judgment, if it is possible to make it at all or if it is useful to make, may well be true. All cultures, it seems clear, are not equally noted for drama: the Hebrews had no drama, unless we count the Book of Job as one, and Chinese drama is a very minor part of Chinese literature. But it is not the purpose of this preface to award literary prizes and demerits. In a very real sense comparing the *Shakuntala* to a play of Shakespeare's is like comparing apples to oranges. Kalidasa's work must be evaluated in terms of the dramatic taste and the dramatic theory of his time. That the Western reader can read and enjoy Kalidasa without difficulty is a tribute to the genius of the poet, but also it is made possible by the historical accident that Sanskrit dramatic theory is close to Western, that is, to Aristotelian. And it is this closeness that makes it easy for us to regard Kalidasa's plays as Oriental variations of a norm we already know. Sanskrit drama, nevertheless, has aims which are subtly different from the aims of drama in the European tradition, and a knowledge of some of these aims enriches our experience of reading Kalidasa's plays. Ironically, the category of Asian drama that has most interested the West in the twentieth century is a drama which has no affinities with ours and which contradicts everything we expect in the theater. This is the drama of Japan, especially the Noh play. It is apparently easier for us to accept the completely different than the partially different.

Before discussing how the aims of Sanskrit drama differ from those of Western we should note one area in which Sanskrit drama closely resembles Greek an area which presents some obstacles to the beginning reader of Greek literature but which soon becomes an asset. Both Sanskrit and Greek drama exist in a complex of mythology which involves gods, demi-gods and men and which is systematic enough in each culture to provide the reader with rich overtones. Even after a desultory reading of just a few Greek works we are aware that when Agamemnon quarrels with Achilles in one work he will eventually be murdered by his wife Clytemnestra in another work and that his son Orestes will avenge him in yet another. We know that Helen of Troy, still beautiful enough to launch a thousand ships, will appear later as the forgiven wife of Menelaus, or that Oedipus, blinded, and mentally and spiritually broken, will nevertheless appear again in a further elaboration of the Theban cycle of Greek myth. Thus, there is an extensive and complicated mass of history and legend which the Greek writers hold in common, and a knowledge of this material makes the particular interpretations of it more meaningful. It is not necessary to know the Theban cycle to be interested in Oedipus and his fate, but we can scarcely avoid learning something about it if we read much, and our knowledge enables us to place the characters in the plays in their proper places in a long poetic history. This is likewise true of the Sanskrit drama, but the mythological system is different. The great early surviving sources for Greek myth are Homer's *Iliad* and *Odyssey*. In India likewise two great epic poems, the *Ramayana* and the *Mahabharata,* embody the legendary history of the Indian people. Like the *Iliad* and the *Odyssey* these works have been pillaged by generations of writers who have—again like the Greek dramatists—been content to stick to the main lines of the story but have added artistic arrangement and spiritual and psychological interpretation. This process is endless. Sartre, Cocteau and Giraudoux, among others, have reinterpreted phases of the Agamemnon and Oedipus cycles for the twentieth century; in India the *Ramayana* is constantly rewritten. This comparison must not be pushed too far: the Indian epics are sacred scripture to the Hindu as the Greek legends are not to us, but both legendary traditions seem perpetually vital. Kalidasa takes a simple and unadorned tale in the *Mahabharata* and makes out of it the sophisticated drama of Shakuntala and King Dushyanta, but by going to the epic for his material he immediately provides the audience with the precise location of this story in the cycle of Indian myth. A single example of this must suffice.

On page 6 the Hermit, pleased that the King has decided to spare the deer, calls him "scion of Puru's race" and prays that be will beget a son. This mention of Puru is calculated to remind the audience of both the ancestry and descendants yet unborn (so far as the play is concerned) of Dushyanta. The audience knows that Dushyanta's ancestry is traced back to the Moon or the lunar dynasty of Indian legend, that one of his ancestors was saved at the time of the deluge by the god Vishnu, and that he is descended from the great King Puru. At the same time the coupling of Puru's name with a pious wish for a male heir for the king reminds the audience that Dushyanta's son will be the great Bharata.

Likewise, Dushyanta, being a pious and god-fearing king, is much concerned with the ancestry of Shakuntala. If she were the wrong caste, he could not marry her. The audience knows of her ancestry and of the religious deeds of her father in the *Ramayana*. Thus, Kalidasa's play, though a love story, is nevertheless firmly fixed in an intricate tradition of sacred legend, and this to the Indian audience provides the same kind of perspective that we get from a scene in which Clytemnestra plays with her children with our knowledge that Orestes and Electra will eventually plot to kill their mother.

To make clear the difference between the Western and the Sanskrit approach to drama we must discuss the place of plot or action in Western drama and the idea of *rasa* ("sympathy" or "flavor") in Sanskrit drama. Both approaches to drama (unlike that of the Japanese Noh play) recognize the need for clearly defined characters in a dramatic conflict. In the case of the love play the hero and the heroine must overcome a certain number of obstacles to achieve their union, and these obstacles should be integrated into a unified plot and not be, in the fashion of soap-opera, a series of unrelated obstacles strung out simply for the purpose of providing new episodes. Thus unity of action is urged, and there is a parallel between Aristotle's idea of unity of time and the Sanskrit doctrine that the events of an act should not exceed a day in duration. However, to Aristotle and to most Western dramatists, including many modern ones, the plot is the soul of the play. Aristotle seems to think that a dramatic effect can be produced even by a summary of the plot, and what we now think of as the "philosophical poem" is not poetry as he defines it. Thus Western drama insofar as it follows this convention is the "imitation of an action" and the characters and their thoughts and feelings are all subordinated to this end. But what is imitated or represented in Sanskrit drama is a state of emotion, and the action, however complicated or exciting it may be, is subordinated to the creation of this state of emotion. The Western drama may be described as a series of minor actions or episodes unified into a major action which is the play; the Sanskrit drama is a series of emotional moods which add up to the dominant emotion of the play. This point may be most positively made with *Shakuntala* by examination of that part of the plot which seems most unreasonable and arbitrary to a Western reader. The curse which the holy man inflicts on Shakuntala seems sudden to us and much too harsh. The shy and naive girl has not deliberately insulted the sage and is certainly deserving of no more than a reprimand. We know that she would respond to a reprimand and correct her error because she is a pious and obedient girl. This episode seems to us to be "overdone" and present in the play to get the plot under way. This criticism would seem not so much incorrect as unimportant to an Indian audience. The purpose of the play is to present to us the varieties of flavor in the emotion of love, and the plot is merely the vehicle for this. We may compare this episode with an emotional scene in a Western dramatist – Shakespeare – whose plays are much less carefully organized than either Sanskrit plays or Greek plays. The death of Falstaff is not integrated with the plot of *Henry V*, however attractive the scene may be and however much we want to know, from having read *Henry IV*, what happened to Falstaff. A Sanskrit critic of this extraneous episode of Shakespeare's would be less concerned with its intrusion into the plot than with whether or not it contributed to the dominant emotion of the play. The comparison should not be forced, needless to say. The sudden intervention of a divine or semi-divine power is certainly more congenial to the Hindu mind than to the Western, and we note the uneasiness of modern critics in the presence of divine intervention in Greek plays. But the essential point is that Sanskrit drama subordinates plot to the depiction of emotional states.

The dominant emotion or *rasa* of *Shakuntala* is the erotic, that is, love in all its phases from the sensual to the spiritual. Sanskrit dramatic theory recognizes a number of legitimate dominant emotions for the playwrights to employ, including categories familar to us such as heroism, mirth, the state of anger, the state of terror and others. These have been elaborately classified and analyzed in treatises on dramatic composition, some of which may antedate Kalidasa. The pervading sentiment of a play is created by a series of emotional states in the acts and scenes, gestures and verses, and the varieties of emotion which can be employed to create one of the dominant emotions have also been elaborately – perhaps too elaborately – classified. The significance of this for the modern reader is that he should savor each scene. He should ask himself what emotional nuance is created here and taste its quality, and not press on too eagerly to unroll the plot.

At the beginning of the play, King Dushyanta descends from the hunting chariot and enters the peace and calm of the hermitage. He immediately feels (page 8) a throbbing in his arm (which he indicates on stage by a gesture). This in Hindu legend is a sign that he will have union with a beautiful woman. However, as he says, a religious hermitage scarcely seems a likely place for an amour, and the king has been reminded that as a member of the royal caste he protects hermitages (the scars from the bowstring on his arm symbolize this). In this Hollywood age of love and romance it is refreshing to find that there are just two simple aspects of King Dushyanta's infatuation with Shakuntala. Her physical attributes–her graceful movements, her face, and her figure–fill him with desire. But Dushyanta is a noble and pious king; the other question is "Can I lawfully have her?" She cannot be pledged either to another or to a lifetime of religious chastity, and she cannot be a member of the wrong caste or a union with her would be immoral. Much of the beauty of Act I of the play is concentrated on the young girl who has just arrived at maturity in the rustic setting of the hermitage. Her shyness and excitement and the sly fun of her attendants on the one hand contrast with the anxieties of the king about her background. To the king, Shakuntala is a lotus leaf, a symbol of beauty, among vines in one verse and among aquatic plants in another. The king protects her, in an idyllic scene, not from brigands but from an attacking bee. By the end of the act Shakuntala has moved to Stage Two of womanhood. She has become sufficiently interested in Dushyanta to pretend to have hurt her foot so as to delay and gain a last glance at the king. There is not the slightest suggestion in the play that Dushyanta and his new love need to be intellectually or emotionally "made for each other"; they do not even need to hold an extended conversation. It is sufficient that he is a noble king and that she has physical beauty and the proper religious background. These facts separate the love affair from the tradition of Western romantic love by a wide gulf. That Dushyanta is much married is also likely to be disturbing to the Western reader. Kalidasa wisely keeps Queen Hansavati from appearing. Her song merely reminds Dushyanta that there is another love in his subconscious mind.

Despite his lack of interest in what in the twentieth century would be called "compatibility," Kalidasa paints a great variety of the aspects of love in *Shakuntala:* the heroine's shyness, the hints of her attendants, the jests (which are never vulgar) of the *vidūṣaka* or clown, the king's interest in her beauty contrasted with his piety and nobility, the king's love for his son, and joy of reunion after a period of suffering for both hero and heroine. The validity of the curse of Durvasas must be accepted, and the last scene in paradise must be recognized as partly symbolic and also as analogous to the Greek tradition of the intervention of gods in human affairs (and occasionally, as in the case of Hercules at the end of the *Philoctetes* of Sophocles, of the god appearing on stage). Throughout *Shakuntala* imagery drawn from nature provides a counterpoint to the affairs of the lovers. In Act IV, for instance, even the trees weep when Shakuntala leaves the hermitage. Much of this love of nature comes through to us, but we must remind ourselves that each phase of the nature imagery has a symbolic value to the Indian audience. There is not space to discuss this here, but one symbol, the lotus, which represents beauty, we have mentioned already.

The other dramas of Kalidasa are not quite up to the level of *Shakuntala,* but are well worth our investigation. *Malavika and Agnimitra* is likewise a love story with the crafty clown in a prominent role. The *vidūsaka's* attempts to bring his master and the beloved together are amusing and will remind readers of certain rascally servants in Western drama. The furious rivalry of the two queens is depicted with grace and delicacy, despite the passions involved. The *Tale of Urvashi Won by Valour* is perhaps too filled with the supernatural for modern taste but in this work we see Kalidasa's imagination at its most fanciful. Urvashi's passion, in fact, might seem excessive if the magical quality of the play did not make her somewhat remote from real life.

Kalidasa's poems will not seem as important to the Western reader as his plays, but they nevertheless reveal his genius as the poet of man in relation to nature. The *Seasons* is a youthful work which relates the varied moods of nature (nature in India, we must remember!) to the loves of boy and girl or husband and wife. The *Cloud-Messenger* seems remote to us because of the celestial atmosphere and because the *yaksha* who is being punished is really divine and cannot be killed or injured as could a mortal man. But the love and longing in the poem are symbolic, on the heavenly plane, of the same experiences in human life. The *Birth of the War-god* has much variety and intensity of feeling and an underlying theme which makes it more pertinent to the mind used to modern literature. The depiction of the love affair of two deities offended some Sanskrit critics just as Plato protested the immorality of the activities of the gods in Greek legend. But the parable in the work is that the forces of procreation are powerful and the gods in the play reveal to us that these forces have divine sanctification. Finally, Kalidasa's epic poem, the *Dynasty of Raghu,* takes as its hero the great Rama of the classical Hindu epic, the *Ramayana,* and is an excellent example of a type of Hindu epic which should be based on traditional themes and promote the virtues of good conduct, worldly success, final release from worldly things, and love.

That love or the erotic *rasa* is an important part of Kalidasa's work may make him seem inferior to Western dramatists and poets who take themes like death, madness, treason and valor. But we must remind ourselves that love and hate, or to put it more mildly, the attraction and repulsion both physical and psychological which exist between every human being and every other human being are much more a part of our daily lives, fortunately, than death, exile, or bloodshed. To descend to modern psychological jargon, Kalidasa is the poet of interpersonal relations. He sees the love of a man for a maid at one end of the emotional spectrum that has at the other end the love of an ascetic for God. Eros is part of Agape and Agape part of Eros in this system. The reader must seek out the precise emotional nuance in each passage of the poet's work to appreciate the variety and depth of Kalidasa's reading of human experience. It is not the end, but the moment, that counts. That Kalidasa is different from Shakespeare is more important than whether he is superior or inferior. The "finest master of Indian poetic style," as Keith calls him, has much to say to the Western reader.

G. L. ANDERSON

New York University
1959

SELECT BIBLIOGRAPHY

Arthur W. Ryder's translation of Kalidasa's works is the best in English, though Monier Williams' translation of *Shakuntala* is satisfactory and Sir William Jones' (1789) is still worth reading. Monier Williams' edition of *Shakuntala* (2nd edition, 1876) has useful notes, though R. Pischel's in the Harvard Oriental Series provides a better text. By far the best study of Sanskrit drama is Arthur B. Keith's *Sanskrit Drama* (1924); Keith's *History of Sanskrit Literature* (1920) discusses Kalidasa's poems.

An interesting general introduction to Indian poetry is Daniel H. H. Ingalls' "Sanskrit Poetry and Sanskrit Poetics" in the University of North Carolina Studies in Comparative Literature, 1955. Studies of Kalidasa abound. Some recent ones are G. C. Jhala, *Kalidasa: A Study* (Bombay, 1943); B. S. Upadhyaya, *India in Kalidasa* (Allahabad, 1947); C. K. Raja, *Kalidasa, a Critical Study* (Waltair, 1956); Walter Ruben, *Kalidasa* (Berlin, 1956); John D. Mitchell, "A Sanskrit Classic: *Shakuntala*" in *Approaches to the Oriental Classics,* edited by W. T. de Bary (New York, 1959).

G.L.A.

*Willst du die Blüthe des frühen, die Früchte des
späteren Jahres,*
*Willst du, was reizt und entzückt, willst du was
sättigt und nährt,*
*Willst du den Himmel, die Erde, mit Einem Namen
begreifen;*
Nenn' ich, Sakuntala, Dich, und so ist Alles gesagt.

GOETHE.

Wouldst thou the young year's blossoms and the
fruits of its decline,
And all by which the soul is charmed, enraptured,
feasted, fed?
Wouldst thou the earth and heaven itself in one
sole name combine?
I name thee, O Shakuntala, and all at once is said.

(Eastwich's translation)

KALIDASA

An ancient heathen poet, loving more
God's creatures, and His women, and His flowers
Than we who boast of consecrated powers;
Still lavishing his unexhausted store

Of love's deep, simple wisdom, healing o'er
The world's old sorrows, India's griefs and ours;
That healing love he found in palace towers,
On mountain, plain, and dark, sea-belted shore,

In songs of holy Raghu's kingly line
Or sweet Shakuntala in pious grove,
In hearts that met where starry jasmines twine

Or hearts that from long, lovelorn absence strove
Together. Still his words of wisdom shine:
All's well with man, when man and woman love.

SHAKUNTALA AND OTHER WRITINGS

SHAKUNTALA

A PLAY IN SEVEN ACTS

DRAMATIS PERSONÆ

KING DUSHYANTA.
BHARATA, *nicknamed* All-tamer, *his son.*
MADHAVYA, *a clown, his companion.*
His charioteer.
RAIVATAKA, *a door-keeper.*
BHADRASENA, *a general.*
KARABHAKA, *a servant.*
PARVATAYANA, *a chamberlain.*
SOMARATA, *a chaplain.*

KANVA, *hermit-father.*
SHARNGARAVA }
SHARADVATA } *his pupils.*
HARITA }
DURVASAS, *an irascible sage.*

The chief of police.
SUCHAKA }
JANUKA } *policemen.*
A fisherman.

SHAKUNTALA, *foster-child of Kanva.*
ANUSUYA }
PRIYAMVADA } *her friends.*
GAUTAMI, *hermit-mother.*

KASHYAPA, *father of the gods.*
ADITI, *mother of the gods.*
MATALI, *charioteer of heaven's king.*
GALAVA, *a pupil in heaven.*
MISHRAKESHI, *a heavenly nymph.*

Stage-director and actress (in the prologue), hermits and hermit-women, two court poets, palace attendants, invisible fairies.

The first four acts pass in Kanva's forest hermitage; acts five and six in the king's palace; act seven on a heavenly mountain. The time is perhaps seven years.

SHAKUNTALA

PROLOGUE

BENEDICTION UPON THE AUDIENCE

Eight forms has Shiva, lord of all and king:
And these are water, first created thing;
And fire, which speeds the sacrifice begun;
The priest; and time's dividers, moon and sun;
The all-embracing ether, path of sound;
The earth, wherein all seeds of life are found;
And air, the breath of life: may he draw near,
Revealed in these, and bless those gathered here.

The stage-director. Enough of this! (*Turning toward the dressing-room.*) Madam, if you are ready, pray come here. (*Enter an actress.*)

Actress. Here I am, sir. What am I to do?

Director. Our audience is very discriminating, and we are to offer them a new play, called *Shakuntala and the ring of recognition,* written by the famous Kalidasa. Every member of the cast must be on his mettle.

Actress. Your arrangements are perfect. Nothing will go wrong.

Director (*smiling*). To tell the truth, madam,

Until the wise are satisfied,
I cannot feel that skill is shown;
The best-trained mind requires support,
And does not trust itself alone.

Actress. True. What shall we do first?

Director. First, you must sing something to please the ears of the audience.

Actress. What season of the year shall I sing about?

Director. Why, sing about the pleasant summer which has just begun. For at this time of year

A mid-day plunge will temper heat;
  The breeze is rich with forest flowers;
To slumber in the shade is sweet;
  And charming are the twilight hours.

Actress (*sings*).

The siris-blossoms fair,
  With pollen laden,
Are plucked to deck her hair
  By many a maiden,
But gently; flowers like these
Are kissed by eager bees.

Director. Well done! The whole theatre is captivated by your song, and sits as if painted. What play shall we give them to keep their good-will?

Actress. Why, you just told me we were to give a new play called *Shakuntala and the ring.*

Director. Thank you for reminding me. For the moment I had quite forgotten.

Your charming song had carried me away
As the deer enticed the hero of our play.

(*Exeunt ambo.*)

ACT I

The Hunt

(*Enter, in a chariot, pursuing a deer,* King Dushyanta, *bow and arrow in hand ; and a charioteer.*)

Charioteer (*looking at the king and the deer*). Your Majesty,

I see you hunt the spotted deer
With shafts to end his race,
As though God Shiva should appear
In his immortal chase.

King. Charioteer, the deer has led us a long chase. And even now

His neck in beauty bends
As backward looks he sends
At my pursuing car
That threatens death from far.
Fear shrinks to half the body small;
See how he fears the arrow's fall!

The path he takes is strewed
With blades of grass half-chewed
From jaws wide with the stress
Of fevered weariness.
He leaps so often and so high,
He does not seem to run, but fly.

(*In surprise.*) Pursue as I may, I can hardly keep him in sight.

Charioteer. Your Majesty, I have been holding the horses back because the ground was rough. This checked us and gave the deer a lead. Now we are on level ground, and you will easily overtake him.

King. Then let the reins hang loose.

Charioteer. Yes, your Majesty. (*He counterfeits rapid motion.*) Look, your Majesty!

The lines hang loose; the steeds unreined
Dart forward with a will.

Their ears are pricked; their necks are strained;
  Their plumes lie straight and still.
They leave the rising dust behind;
They seem to float upon the wind.

King (*joyfully*). See! The horses are gaining on the deer.

As onward and onward the chariot flies,
The small flashes large to my dizzy eyes.
What is cleft in twain, seems to blur and mate;
What is crooked in nature, seems to be straight.
Things at my side in an instant appear
Distant, and things in the distance, near.

A voice behind the scenes. O King, this deer belongs to the hermitage, and must not be killed.

Charioteer (*listening and looking*). Your Majesty, here are two hermits, come to save the deer at the moment when your arrow was about to fall.

King (*hastily*). Stop the chariot.

Charioteer. Yes, your Majesty. (*He does so. Enter a hermit with his pupil.*)

Hermit (*lifting his hand*). O King, this deer belongs to the hermitage.

Why should his tender form expire,
As blossoms perish in the fire?
How could that gentle life endure
The deadly arrow, sharp and sure?

Restore your arrow to the quiver;
  To you were weapons lent
The broken-hearted to deliver,
  Not strike the innocent.

King (*bowing low*). It is done. (*He does so.*)

Hermit (*joyfully*). A deed worthy of you, scion of Puru's race, and shining example of kings. May you beget a son to rule earth and heaven.

King (*bowing low*). I am thankful for a Brahman's blessing.

The two hermits. O King, we are on our way to gather firewood. Here, along the bank of the Malini, you may see the hermitage of Father Kanva, over which Shakuntala presides, so to speak, as guardian deity. Unless other duties prevent, pray enter here and receive a welcome. Besides,

Beholding pious hermit-rites
Preserved from fearful harm,
Perceive the profit of the scars
On your protecting arm.

King. Is the hermit father there?

The two hermits. No, he has left his daughter to welcome guests, and has just gone to Somatirtha, to avert an evil fate that threatens her.

King. Well, I will see her. She shall feel my devotion, and report it to the sage.

The two hermits. Then we will go on our way. (*Exit hermit with pupil.*)

King. Charioteer, drive on. A sight of the pious hermitage will purify us.

Charioteer. Yes, your Majesty. (*He counterfeits motion again.*)

King (*looking about*). One would know, without being told, that this is the precinct of a pious grove.

Charioteer. How so?

King. Do you not see? Why, here

Are rice-grains, dropped from bills of parrot chicks
Beneath the trees; and pounding-stones where sticks
A little almond-oil; and trustful deer
That do not run away as we draw near;
And river-paths that are besprinkled yet
From trickling hermit-garments, clean and wet.

Besides,

The roots of trees are washed by many a stream
That breezes ruffle; and the flowers' red gleam
Is dimmed by pious smoke; and fearless fawns
Move softly on the close-cropped forest lawns.

Charioteer. It is all true.

King (*after a little*). We must not disturb the hermitage. Stop here while I dismount.

Charioteer. I am holding the reins. Dismount, your Majesty.

King (*dismounts and looks at himself*). One should wear modest garments on entering a hermitage. Take these jewels and the bow. (*He gives them to the charioteer.*) Before

I return from my visit to the hermits, have the horses' backs wet down.

Charioteer. Yes, your Majesty. (*Exit.*)

King (*walking and looking about*). The hermitage! Well, I will enter. (*As he does so, he feels a throbbing in his arm.*)

A tranquil spot! Why should I thrill?
  Love cannot enter there—
Yet to inevitable things
  Doors open everywhere.

A voice behind the scenes. This way, girls!

King (*listening*). I think I hear some one to the right of the grove. I must find out. (*He walks and looks about.*) Ah, here are hermit-girls, with watering-pots just big enough for them to handle. They are coming in this direction to water the young trees. They are charming!

The city maids, for all their pains,
  Seem not so sweet and good;
Our garden blossoms yield to these
  Flower-children of the wood.

I will draw back into the shade and wait for them. (*He stands, gazing toward them. Enter* SHAKUNTALA, *as described, and her two friends.*)

First friend. It seems to me, dear, that Father Kanva cares more for the hermitage trees than he does for you. You are delicate as a jasmine blossom, yet he tells you to fill the trenches about the trees.

Shakuntala. Oh, it isn't Father's bidding so much. I feel like a real sister to them. (*She waters the trees.*)

Priyamvada. Shakuntala, we have watered the trees that blossom in the summer-time. Now let's sprinkle those whose flowering-time is past. That will be a better deed, because we shall not be working for a reward.

Shakuntala. What a pretty idea! (*She does so.*)

King (*to himself*). And this is Kanva's daughter, Shakuntala. (*In surprise.*) The good Father does wrong to make her wear the hermit's dress of bark.

The sage who yokes her artless charm
  With pious pain and grief,
Would try to cut the toughest vine
  With a soft, blue lotus-leaf.

Well, I will step behind a tree and see how she acts with her friends. (*He conceals himself.*)

Shakuntala. Oh, Anusuya! Priyamvada has fastened this bark dress so tight that it hurts. Please loosen it. (ANUSUYA *does so.*)

Priyamvada (laughing). You had better blame your own budding charms for that.

King. She is quite right.

Beneath the barken dress
  Upon the shoulder tied,
In maiden loveliness
  Her young breast seems to hide,

As when a flower amid
  The leaves by autumn tossed—
Pale, withered leaves—lies hid,
  And half its grace is lost.

Yet in truth the bark dress is not an enemy to her beauty. It serves as an added ornament. For

The meanest vesture glows
  On beauty that enchants:
The lotus lovelier shows
  Amid dull water-plants;

The moon in added splendour
  Shines for its spot of dark;
Yet more the maiden slender
  Charms in her dress of bark.

Shakuntala (looking ahead). Oh, girls, that mango-tree is trying to tell me something with his branches that move in the wind like fingers. I must go and see him. (*She does so.*)

Priyamvada. There, Shakuntala, stand right where you are a minute.

Shakuntala. Why?

Priyamvada. When I see you there, it looks as if a vine were clinging to the mango-tree.

Shakuntala. I see why they call you the flatterer.

King. But the flattery is true.

Her arms are tender shoots; her lips
 Are blossoms red and warm;
Bewitching youth begins to flower
 In beauty on her form.

Anusuya. Oh, Shakuntala! Here is the jasmine-vine that you named Light of the Grove. She has chosen the mango-tree as her husband.

Shakuntala (*approaches and looks at it, joyfully*). What a pretty pair they make. The jasmine shows her youth in her fresh flowers, and the mango-tree shows his strength in his ripening fruit. (*She stands gazing at them.*)

Priyamvada (*smiling*). Anusuya, do you know why Shakuntala looks so hard at the Light of the Grove?

Anusuya. No. Why?

Priyamvada. She is thinking how the Light of the Grove has found a good tree, and hoping that she will meet a fine lover.

Shakuntala. That's what you want for yourself. (*She tips her watering-pot.*)

Anusuya. Look, Shakuntala! Here is the spring-creeper that Father Kanva tended with his own hands—just as he did you. You are forgetting her.

Shakuntala. I'd forget myself sooner. (*She goes to the creeper and looks at it, joyfully.*) Wonderful! Wonderful! Priyamvada, I have something pleasant to tell you.

Priyamvada. What is it, dear?

Shakuntala. It is out of season, but the spring-creeper is covered with buds down to the very root.

The two friends (*running up*). Really?

Shakuntala. Of course. Can't you see?

Priyamvada (*looking at it joyfully*). And I have something pleasant to tell *you*. You are to be married soon.

Shakuntala (*snappishly*). You know that's just what you want for yourself.

Priyamvada. I'm not teasing. I really heard Father Kanva say that this flowering vine was to be a symbol of your coming happiness.

Anusuya. Priyamvada, that is why Shakuntala waters the spring-creeper so lovingly.

Shakuntala. She is my sister. Why shouldn't I give her water? (*She tips her watering-pot.*)

King. May I hope that she is the hermit's daughter by a mother of a different caste? But it *must* be so.

Surely, she may become a warrior's bride;
Else, why these longings in an honest mind?
The motions of a blameless heart decide
Of right and wrong, when reason leaves us blind.

Yet I will learn the whole truth.

Shakuntala (*excitedly*). Oh, oh! A bee has left the jasmine-vine and is flying into my face. (*She shows herself annoyed by the bee.*)

King (*ardently*).

As the bee about her flies,
Swiftly her bewitching eyes
Turn to watch his flight.
She is practising to-day
Coquetry and glances' play
Not from love, but fright.

(*Jealously.*)

Eager bee, you lightly skim
O'er the eyelid's trembling rim
Toward the cheek aquiver.
Gently buzzing round her cheek,
Whispering in her ear, you seek
Secrets to deliver.

While her hands that way and this
Strike at you, you steal a kiss,
Love's all, honeymaker.
I know nothing but her name,
Not her caste, nor whence she came—
You, my rival, take her.

Shakuntala. Oh, girls! Save me from this dreadful bee!

The two friends (*smiling*). Who are we, that we should save you? Call upon Dushyanta. For pious groves are in the protection of the king.

King. A good opportunity to present myself. Have no— (*He checks himself. Aside.*) No, they would see that I am the king. I prefer to appear as a guest.

Shakuntala. He doesn't leave me alone! I am going to

run away. (*She takes a step and looks about.*) Oh, dear! Oh, dear! He is following me. Please save me.

King (*hastening forward*). Ah!

A king of Puru's mighty line
  Chastises shameless churls;
What insolent is he who baits
  These artless hermit-girls?

(*The girls are a little flurried on seeing the king.*)

Anusuya. It is nothing very dreadful, sir. But our friend (*indicating* SHAKUNTALA) was teased and frightened by a bee.

King (*to* SHAKUNTALA). I hope these pious days are happy ones. (SHAKUNTALA'S *eyes drop in embarrassment.*)

Anusuya. Yes, now that we receive such a distinguished guest.

Priyamvada. Welcome, sir. Go to the cottage, Shakuntala, and bring fruit. This water will do to wash the feet.

King. Your courteous words are enough to make me feel at home.

Anusuya. Then, sir, pray sit down and rest on this shady bench.

King. You, too, are surely wearied by your pious task. Pray be seated a moment.

Priyamvada (*aside to* SHAKUNTALA). My dear, we must be polite to our guest. Shall we sit down? (*The three girls sit.*)

Shakuntala (*to herself*). Oh, why do I have such feelings when I see this man? They seem wrong in a hermitage.

King (*looking at the girls*). It is delightful to see your friendship. For you are all young and beautiful.

Priyamvada (*aside to* ANUSUYA). Who is he, dear? With his mystery, and his dignity, and his courtesy? He acts like a king and a gentleman.

Anusuya. I am curious too. I am going to ask him. (*Aloud.*) Sir, you are so very courteous that I make bold to ask you something. What royal family do you adorn, sir? What country is grieving at your absence? Why does a gentleman so delicately bred submit to the weary journey into our pious grove?

Shakuntala (*aside*). Be brave, my heart. Anusuya speaks your very thoughts.

King (*aside*). Shall I tell at once who I am, or conceal it? (*He reflects.*) This will do. (*Aloud.*) I am a student of Scripture. It is my duty to see justice done in the cities of the king. And I have come to this hermitage on a tour of inspection.

Anusuya. Then we of the hermitage have some one to take care of us. (SHAKUNTALA *shows embarrassment.*)

The two friends (*observing the demeanour of the pair. Aside to* SHAKUNTALA). Oh, Shakuntala! If only Father were here to-day.

Shakuntala. What would he do?

The two friends. He would make our distinguished guest happy, if it took his most precious treasure.

Shakuntala (*feigning anger*). Go away! You mean something. I'll not listen to you.

King. I too would like to ask a question about your friend.

The two friends. Sir, your request is a favour to us.

King. Father Kanva lives a lifelong hermit. Yet you say that your friend is his daughter. How can that be?

Anusuya. Listen, sir. There is a majestic royal sage named Kaushika——

King. Ah, yes. The famous Kaushika.

Anusuya. Know, then, that he is the source of our friend's being. But Father Kanva is her real father, because he took care of her when she was abandoned.

King. You waken my curiosity with the word "abandoned." May I hear the whole story?

Anusuya. Listen, sir. Many years ago, that royal sage was leading a life of stern austerities, and the gods, becoming strangely jealous, sent the nymph Menaka to disturb his devotions.

King. Yes, the gods feel this jealousy toward the austerities of others. And then——

Anusuya. Then in the lovely spring-time he saw her intoxicating beauty—— (*She stops in embarrassment.*)

King. The rest is plain. Surely, she is the daughter of the nymph.

Anusuya. Yes.

King. It is as it should be.

To beauty such as this
  No woman could give birth;
The quivering lightning flash
  Is not a child of earth.

(SHAKUNTALA *hangs her head in confusion.*)

King (*to himself*). Ah, my wishes become hopes.

Priyamvada (*looking with a smile at* SHAKUNTALA). Sir, it seems as if you had more to say. (SHAKUNTALA *threatens her friend with her finger.*)

King. You are right. Your pious life interests me, and I have another question.

Priyamvada. Do not hesitate. We hermit people stand ready to answer all demands.

King. My question is this:

Does she, till marriage only, keep her vow
  As hermit-maid, that shames the ways of love?
Or must her soft eyes ever see, as now,
  Soft eyes of friendly deer in peaceful grove?

Priyamvada. Sir, we are under bonds to lead a life of virtue. But it is her father's wish to give her to a suitable lover.

King (*joyfully to himself*).

O heart, your wish is won!
All doubt at last is done;
The thing you feared as fire,
Is the jewel of your desire.

Shakuntala (*pettishly*). Anusuya, I'm going.

Anusuya. What for?

Shakuntala. I am going to tell Mother Gautami that Priyamvada is talking nonsense. (*She rises.*)

Anusuya. My dear, we hermit people cannot neglect to entertain a distinguished guest, and go wandering about.

(SHAKUNTALA *starts to walk away without answering.*)

King (*aside*). She is going! (*He starts up as if to detain her, then checks his desires.*) A thought is as vivid as an act, to a lover.

Though nurture, conquering nature, holds
  Me back, it seems
As had I started and returned
  In waking dreams.

Priyamvada (*approaching* SHAKUNTALA). You dear, peevish girl! You mustn't go.

Shakuntala (*turns with a frown*). Why not?

Priyamvada. You owe me the watering of two trees. You

can go when you have paid your debt. (*She forces her to come back.*)

King. It is plain that she is already wearied by watering the trees. See!

Her shoulders droop; her palms are reddened yet;
  Quick breaths are struggling in her bosom fair;
The blossom o'er her ear hangs limply wet;
  One hand restrains the loose, dishevelled hair.

I therefore remit her debt. (*He gives the two friends a ring. They take it, read the name engraved on it, and look at each other.*)

King. Make no mistake. This is a present—from the king.

Priyamvada. Then, sir, you ought not to part with it. Your word is enough to remit the debt.

Anusuya. Well, Shakuntala, you are set free by this kind gentleman—or rather, by the king himself. Where are you going now?

Shakuntala (*to herself*). I would never leave him if I could help myself.

Priyamvada. Why don't you go now?

Shakuntala. I am not *your* servant any longer. I will go when I like.

King (*looking at* SHAKUNTALA. *To himself*). Does she feel toward me as I do toward her? At least, there is ground for hope.

Although she does not speak to me,
  She listens while I speak;
Her eyes turn not to see my face,
  But nothing else they seek.

A voice behind the scenes. Hermits! Hermits! Prepare to defend the creatures in our pious grove. King Dushyanta is hunting in the neighbourhood.

The dust his horses' hoofs have raised,
  Red as the evening sky,
Falls like a locust-swarm on boughs
  Where hanging garments dry.

King (*aside*). Alas! My soldiers are disturbing the pious grove in their search for me.

The voice behind the scenes. Hermits! Hermits! Here is an elephant who is terrifying old men, women, and children.

One tusk is splintered by a cruel blow
Against a blocking tree; his gait is slow,
For countless fettering vines impede and cling;
He puts the deer to flight; some evil thing
He seems, that comes our peaceful life to mar,
Fleeing in terror from the royal car.

(*The girls listen and rise anxiously.*)

King. I have offended sadly against the hermits. I must go back.

The two friends. Your Honour, we are frightened by this alarm of the elephant. Permit us to return to the cottage.

Anusuya (*to* SHAKUNTALA). Shakuntala dear, Mother Gautami will be anxious. We must hurry and find her.

Shakuntala (*feigning lameness*). Oh, oh! I can hardly walk.

King. You must go very slowly. And I will take pains that the hermitage is not disturbed.

The two friends. Your honour, we feel as if we knew you very well. Pray pardon our shortcomings as hostesses. May we ask you to seek better entertainment from us another time?

King. You are too modest. I feel honoured by the mere sight of you.

Shakuntala. Anusuya, my foot is cut on a sharp blade of grass, and my dress is caught on an amaranth twig. Wait for me while I loosen it. (*She casts a lingering glance at the king, and goes out with her two friends.*)

King (*sighing*). They are gone. And I must go. The sight of Shakuntala has made me dread the return to the city. I will make my men camp at a distance from the pious grove. But I cannot turn my own thoughts from Shakuntala.

It is my body leaves my love, not I;
  My body moves away, but not my mind;
For back to her my struggling fancies fly
  Like silken banners borne against the wind. (*Exit.*)

ACT II

The Secret

(*Enter the clown.*)

Clown (*sighing*). Damn! Damn! Damn! I'm tired of being friends with this sporting king. "There's a deer!" he shouts, "There's a boar!" And off he chases on a summer noon through woods where shade is few and far between. We drink hot, stinking water from the mountain streams, flavoured with leaves—nasty! At odd times we get a little tepid meat to eat. And the horses and the elephants make such a noise that I can't even be comfortable at night. Then the hunters and the bird-chasers—damn 'em—wake me up bright and early. They do make an ear-splitting rumpus when they start for the woods. But even that isn't the whole misery. There's a new pimple growing on the old boil. He left us behind and went hunting a deer. And there in a hermitage they say he found—oh, dear! oh, dear! he found a hermit-girl named Shakuntala. Since then he hasn't a thought of going back to town. I lay awake all night, thinking about it. What can I do? Well, I'll see my friend when he is dressed and beautified. (*He walks and looks about.*) Hello! Here he comes, with his bow in his hand, and his girl in his heart. He is wearing a wreath of wild flowers! I'll pretend to be all knocked up. Perhaps I can get a rest that way. (*He stands, leaning on his staff. Enter the king, as described.*)

King (*to himself*).

Although my darling is not lightly won,
  She seemed to love me, and my hopes are bright;
Though love be balked ere joy be well begun,
  A common longing is itself delight.

(*Smiling.*) Thus does a lover deceive himself. He judges his love's feelings by his own desires.

Her glance was loving—but 'twas not for me;
Her step was slow—'twas grace, not coquetry;
Her speech was short—to her detaining friend.
In things like these love reads a selfish end!

Clown (*standing as before*). Well, king, I can't move my hand. I can only greet you with my voice.

King (*looking and smiling*). What makes you lame?

Clown. Good! You hit a man in the eye, and then ask him why the tears come.

King. I do not understand you. Speak plainly.

Clown. When a reed bends over like a hunchback, do you blame the reed or the river-current?

King. The river-current, of course.

Clown. And you are to blame for my troubles.

King. How so?

Clown. It's a fine thing for you to neglect your royal duties and such a sure job—to live in the woods! What's the good of talking? Here I am, a Brahman, and my joints are all shaken up by this eternal running after wild animals, so that I can't move. Please be good to me. Let us have a rest for just one day.

King (*to himself*). He says this. And I too, when I remember Kanva's daughter, have little desire for the chase. For

The bow is strung, its arrow near;
  And yet I cannot bend
That bow against the fawns who share
  Soft glances with their friend.

Clown (*observing the king*). He means more than he says. I might as well weep in the woods.

King (*smiling*). What more could I mean? I have been thinking that I ought to take my friend's advice.

Clown (*cheerfully*). Long life to you, then. (*He unstiffens.*)

King. Wait. Hear me out.

Clown. Well, sir?

King. When you are rested, you must be my companion in another task—an easy one.

Clown. Crushing a few sweetmeats?

King. I will tell you presently.

Clown. Pray command my leisure.

King. Who stands without? (*Enter the door-keeper.*)

Door-keeper. I await your Majesty's commands.

King. Raivataka, summon the general.

Door-keeper. Yes, your Majesty. (*He goes out, then returns with the general.*) Follow me, sir. There is his Majesty, listening to our conversation. Draw near, sir.

General (*observing the king, to himself*). Hunting is declared to be a sin, yet it brings nothing but good to the king. See!

He does not heed the cruel sting
Of his recoiling, twanging string;
The mid-day sun, the dripping sweat
Affect him not, nor make him fret;
His form, though sinewy and spare,
Is most symmetrically fair;
No mountain-elephant could be
More filled with vital strength than he.

(*He approaches.*) Victory to your Majesty! The forest is full of deer-tracks, and beasts of prey cannot be far off. What better occupation could we have?

King. Bhadrasena, my enthusiasm is broken. Madhavya has been preaching against hunting.

General (*aside to the clown*). Stick to it, friend Madhavya. I will humour the king a moment. (*Aloud.*) Your Majesty, he is a chattering idiot. Your Majesty may judge by his own case whether hunting is an evil. Consider:

The hunter's form grows sinewy, strong, and light;
He learns, from beasts of prey, how wrath and fright
Affect the mind; his skill he loves to measure
With moving targets. 'Tis life's chiefest pleasure.

Clown (*angrily*). Get out! Get out with your strenuous life! The king has come to his senses. But you, you son of a slave-wench, can go chasing from forest to forest, till you fall into the jaws of some old bear that is looking for a deer or a jackal.

King. Bhadrasena, I cannot take your advice, because I am in the vicinity of a hermitage. So for to-day

The hornèd buffalo may shake
The turbid water of the lake;

Shade-seeking deer may chew the cud,
Boars trample swamp-grass in the mud;
The bow I bend in hunting, may
Enjoy a listless holiday.

General. Yes, your Majesty.

King. Send back the archers who have gone ahead. And forbid the soldiers to vex the hermitage, or even to approach it. Remember:

There lurks a hidden fire in each
  Religious hermit-bower;
Cool sun-stones kindle if assailed
  By any foreign power.

General. Yes, your Majesty.

Clown. Now will you get out with your strenuous life? (*Exit general.*)

King (*to his attendants*). Lay aside your hunting dress. And you, Raivataka, return to your post of duty.

Raivataka. Yes, your Majesty. (*Exit.*)

Clown. You have got rid of the vermin. Now be seated on this flat stone, over which the trees spread their canopy of shade. I can't sit down till you do.

King. Lead the way.

Clown. Follow me. (*They walk about and sit down.*)

King. Friend Madhavya, you do not know what vision is. You have not seen the fairest of all objects.

Clown. I see you, right in front of me.

King. Yes, every one thinks himself beautiful. But I was speaking of Shakuntala, the ornament of the hermitage.

Clown (*to himself*). I mustn't add fuel to the flame. (*Aloud.*) But you can't have her because she is a hermit-girl. What is the use of seeing her?

King. Fool!

And is it selfish longing then,
  That draws our souls on high
Through eyes that have forgot to wink,
  As the new moon climbs the sky?

Besides, Dushyanta's thoughts dwell on no forbidden object.

Clown. Well, tell me about her.

King. Sprung from a nymph of heaven
Wanton and gay,
Who spurned the blessing given,
Going her way;

By the stern hermit taken
In her most need:
So fell the blossom shaken,
Flower on a weed.

Clown (*laughing*). You are like a man who gets tired of good dates and longs for sour tamarind. All the pearls of the palace are yours, and you want this girl!

King. My friend, you have not seen her, or you could not talk so.

Clown. She must be charming if she surprises *you*.

King. Oh, my friend, she needs not many words.

She is God's vision, of pure thought
Composed in His creative mind;
His reveries of beauty wrought
The peerless pearl of womankind.
So plays my fancy when I see
How great is God, how lovely she.

Clown. How the women must hate her!

King. This too is in my thought.

She seems a flower whose fragrance none has tasted,
A gem uncut by workman's tool,
A branch no desecrating hands have wasted,
Fresh honey, beautifully cool.

No man on earth deserves to taste her beauty,
Her blameless loveliness and worth,
Unless he has fulfilled man's perfect duty—
And is there such a one on earth?

Clown. Marry her quick, then, before the poor girl falls into the hands of some oily-headed hermit.

King. She is dependent on her father, and he is not here.

Clown. But how does she feel toward you?

King. My friend, hermit-girls are by their very nature timid. And yet

When I was near, she could not look at me;
  She smiled—but not to me—and half denied it;
She would not show her love for modesty,
  Yet did not try so very hard to hide it.

Clown. Did you want her to climb into your lap the first time she saw you?

King. But when she went away with her friends, she almost showed that she loved me.

When she had hardly left my side,
"I cannot walk," the maiden cried,
And turned her face, and feigned to free
The dress not caught upon the tree.

Clown. She has given you some memories to chew on. I suppose that is why you are so in love with the pious grove.

King. My friend, think of some pretext under which we may return to the hermitage.

Clown. What pretext do you need? Aren't you the king?

King. What of that?

Clown. Collect the taxes on the hermits' rice.

King. Fool! It is a very different tax which these hermits pay—one that outweighs heaps of gems.

The wealth we take from common men,
  Wastes while we cherish;
These share with us such holiness
  As ne'er can perish.

Voices behind the scenes. Ah, we have found him.

King (*listening*). The voices are grave and tranquil. These must be hermits. (*Enter the door-keeper.*)

Door-keeper. Victory, O King. There are two hermit-youths at the gate.

King. Bid them enter at once.

Door-keeper. Yes, your Majesty. (*He goes out, then returns with the youths.*) Follow me.

First youth (*looking at the king*). A majestic presence, yet it inspires confidence. Nor is this wonderful in a king who is half a saint. For to him

The splendid palace serves as hermitage;
His royal government, courageous, sage,
Adds daily to his merit; it is given
To him to win applause from choirs of heaven
Whose anthems to his glory rise and swell,
Proclaiming him a king, and saint as well.

Second youth. My friend, is this Dushyanta, friend of Indra?

First youth. It is.

Second youth.

Nor is it wonderful that one whose arm
Might bolt a city gate, should keep from harm
The whole broad earth dark-belted by the sea;
For when the gods in heaven with demons fight,
Dushyanta's bow and Indra's weapon bright
Are their reliance for the victory.

The two youths (*approaching*). Victory, O King!

King (*rising*). I salute you.

The two youths. All hail! (*They offer fruit.*)

King (*receiving it and bowing low*). May I know the reason of your coming?

The two youths. The hermits have learned that you are here, and they request——

King. They command rather.

The two youths. The powers of evil disturb our pious life in the absence of the hermit-father. We therefore ask that you will remain a few nights with your charioteer to protect the hermitage.

King. I shall be most happy to do so.

Clown (*to the king*). You rather seem to like being collared this way.

King. Raivataka, tell my charioteer to drive up, and to bring the bow and arrows.

Raivataka. Yes, your Majesty. (*Exit.*)

The two youths.

Thou art a worthy scion of
The kings who ruled our nation
And found, defending those in need,
Their truest consecration.

King. Pray go before. And I will follow straightway.

The two youths. Victory, O King! (*Exeunt.*)

King. Madhavya, have you no curiosity to see Shakuntala?

Clown. I *did* have an unending curiosity, but this talk about the powers of evil has put an end to it.

King. Do not fear. You will be with me.

Clown. I'll stick close to your chariot-wheel. (*Enter the door-keeper.*)

Door-keeper. Your Majesty, the chariot is ready, and awaits your departure to victory. But one Karabhaka has come from the city, a messenger from the queen-mother.

King (*respectfully*). Sent by my mother?

Door-keeper. Yes.

King. Let him enter.

Door-keeper (*goes out and returns with* KARABHAKA). Karabhaka, here is his Majesty. You may draw near.

Karabhaka (*approaching and bowing low*). Victory to your Majesty. The queen-mother sends her commands——

King. What are her commands?

Karabhaka. She plans to end a fasting ceremony on the fourth day from to-day. And on that occasion her dear son must not fail to wait upon her.

King. On the one side is my duty to the hermits, on the other my mother's command. Neither may be disregarded. What is to be done?

Clown (*laughing*). Stay half-way between, like Trishanku.

King. In truth, I am perplexed.

Two inconsistent duties sever
My mind with cruel shock,
As when the current of a river
Is split upon a rock.

(*He reflects.*) My friend, the queen-mother has always felt toward you as toward a son. Do you return, tell her what duty keeps me here, and yourself perform the offices of a son.

Clown. You don't think I am afraid of the devils?

King (*smiling*). O mighty Brahman, who could suspect it?

Clown. But I want to travel like a prince.

King. I will send all the soldiers with you, for the pious grove must not be disturbed.

Clown (*strutting*). Aha! Look at the heir-apparent!

King (*to himself*). The fellow is a chatterbox. He might betray my longing to the ladies of the palace. Good, then! (*He takes the clown by the hand. Aloud.*) Friend Madhavya, my reverence for the hermits draws me to the hermitage. Do not think that I am really in love with the hermit-girl. Just think:

A king, and a girl of the calm hermit-grove,
Bred with the fawns, and a stranger to love!
Then do not imagine a serious quest;
The light words I uttered were spoken in jest.

Clown. Oh, I understand that well enough.

(*Exeunt ambo.*)

ACT III

The Love-making

(Enter a pupil, with sacred grass for the sacrifice.)

Pupil (with meditative astonishment). How great is the power of King Dushyanta! Since his arrival our rites have been undisturbed.

He does not need to bend the bow;
  For every evil thing,
Awaiting not the arrow, flees
  From the twanging of the string.

Well, I will take this sacred grass to the priests, to strew the altar. *(He walks and looks about, then speaks to some one not visible.)* Priyamvada, for whom are you carrying this cuscus-salve and the fibrous lotus-leaves? *(He listens.)* What do you say? That Shakuntala has become seriously ill from the heat, and that these things are to relieve her suffering? Give her the best of care, Priyamvada. She is the very life of the hermit-father. And I will give Gautami the holy water for her. *(Exit. Enter the lovelorn king.)*

King (with a meditative sigh).

I know that stern religion's power
  Keeps guardian watch my maiden o'er;
Yet all my heart flows straight to her
  Like water to the valley-floor.

Oh, mighty Love, thine arrows are made of flowers. How can they be so sharp? *(He recalls something.)* Ah, I understand.

Shiva's devouring wrath still burns in thee,
As burns the eternal fire beneath the sea;
  Else how couldst thou, thyself long since consumed,
Kindle the fire that flames so ruthlessly?

Indeed, the moon and thou inspire confidence, only to deceive the host of lovers.

Thy shafts are blossoms; coolness streams
 From moon-rays: thus the poets sing;
But to the lovelorn, falsehood seems
 To lurk in such imagining;
The moon darts fire from frosty beams;
 Thy flowery arrows cut and sting.

And yet

If Love will trouble her
 Whose great eyes madden me,
I greet him unafraid,
 Though wounded ceaselessly.

O mighty god, wilt thou not show me mercy after such reproaches?

With tenderness unending
 I cherished thee when small,
In vain—thy bow is bending;
 On me thine arrows fall.
My care for thee to such a plight
Has brought me; and it serves me right.

I have driven off the powers of evil, and the hermits have dismissed me. Where shall I go now to rest from my weariness? (*He sighs.*) There is no rest for me except in seeing her whom I love. (*He looks up.*) She usually spends these hours of midday heat with her friends on the vine-wreathed banks of the Malini. I will go there. (*He walks and looks about.*) I believe the slender maiden has just passed through this corridor of young trees. For

The stems from which she gathered flowers
 Are still unhealed;
The sap where twigs were broken off
 Is uncongealed.

(*He feels a breeze stirring.*) This is a pleasant spot, with the wind among the trees.

Limbs that love's fever seizes,
 Their fervent welcome pay
To lotus-fragrant breezes
 That bear the river-spray.

(*He studies the ground.*) Ah, Shakuntala must be in this reedy bower. For

In white sand at the door
  Fresh footprints appear,
The toe lightly outlined,
  The heel deep and clear.

I will hide among the branches, and see what happens. (*He does so. Joyfully.*) Ah, my eyes have found their heaven. Here is the darling of my thoughts, lying upon a flower-strewn bench of stone, and attended by her two friends. I will hear what they say to each other. (*He stands gazing. Enter* SHAKUNTALA *with her two friends.*)

The two friends (*fanning her*). Do you feel better, dear, when we fan you with these lotus-leaves?

Shakuntala (*wearily*). Oh, are you fanning me, my dear girls? (*The two friends look sorrowfully at each other.*)

King. She is seriously ill. (*Doubtfully.*) Is it the heat, or is it as I hope? (*Decidedly.*) It *must* be so.

With salve upon her breast,
  With loosened lotus-chain,
My darling, sore oppressed,
  Is lovely in her pain.

Though love and summer heat
  May work an equal woe,
No maiden seems so sweet
  When summer lays her low.

Priyamvada (*aside to* ANUSUYA). Anusuya, since she first saw the good king, she has been greatly troubled. I do not believe her fever has any other cause.

Anusuya. I suspect you are right. I am going to ask her. My dear, I must ask you something. You are in a high fever.

King. It is too true.

Her lotus-chains that were as white
As moonbeams shining in the night,
Betray the fever's awful pain,
And fading, show a darker stain.

Shakuntala (*half rising.*) Well, say whatever you like.

Anusuya. Shakuntala dear, you have not told us what is going on in your mind. But I have heard old, romantic stories, and I can't help thinking that you are in a state like that of a lady in love. Please tell us what hurts you. We have to understand the disease before we can even try to cure it.

King. Anusuya expresses my own thoughts.

Shakuntala. It hurts me terribly. I can't tell you all at once.

Priyamvada. Anusuya is right, dear. Why do you hide your trouble? You are wasting away every day. You are nothing but a beautiful shadow.

King. Priyamvada is right. See!

Her cheeks grow thin; her breast and shoulders fail;
Her waist is weary and her face is pale:
She fades for love; oh, pitifully sweet!
As vine-leaves wither in the scorching heat.

Shakuntala (sighing). I could not tell any one else. But I shall be a burden to you.

The two friends. That is why we insist on knowing, dear. Grief must be shared to be endured.

King. To friends who share her joy and grief
She tells what sorrow laid her here;
She turned to look her love again
When first I saw her—yet I fear!

Shakuntala. Ever since I saw the good king who protects the pious grove—— (*She stops and fidgets.*)

The two friends. Go on, dear.

Shakuntala. I love him, and it makes me feel like this.

The two friends. Good, good! You have found a lover worthy of your devotion. But of course, a great river always runs into the sea.

King (joyfully). I have heard what I longed to hear.

'Twas love that caused the burning pain;
'Tis love that eases it again;
As when, upon a sultry day,
Rain breaks, and washes grief away.

Shakuntala. Then, if you think best, make the good king take pity upon me. If not, remember that I was.

King. Her words end all doubt.

Priyamvada (aside to ANUSUYA). Anusuya, she is far gone in love and cannot endure any delay.

Anusuya. Priyamvada, can you think of any scheme by which we could carry out her wishes quickly and secretly?

Priyamvada. We must plan about the "secretly." The "quickly" is not hard.

Anusuya. How so?

Priyamvada. Why, the good king shows his love for her in his tender glances, and he has been wasting away, as if he were losing sleep.

King. It is quite true.

> The hot tears, flowing down my cheek
> All night on my supporting arm
> And on its golden bracelet, seek
> To stain the gems and do them harm.
>
> The bracelet slipping o'er the scars
> Upon the wasted arm, that show
> My deeds in hunting and in wars,
> All night is moving to and fro.

Priyamvada (reflecting). Well, she must write him a love-letter. And I will hide it in a bunch of flowers and see that it gets into the king's hand as if it were a relic of the sacrifice.

Anusuya. It is a pretty plan, dear, and it pleases me. What does Shakuntala say?

Shakuntala. I suppose I must obey orders.

Priyamvada. Then compose a pretty little love-song, with a hint of yourself in it.

Shakuntala. I'll try. But my heart trembles, for fear he will despise me.

King.

> Here stands the eager lover, and you pale
> For fear lest he disdain a love so kind:
> The seeker may find fortune, or may fail;
> But how could fortune, seeking, fail to find?

And again:

> The ardent lover comes, and yet you fear
> Lest he disdain love's tribute, were it brought,

The hope of which has led his footsteps here—
  Pearls need not seek, for they themselves are sought.

The two friends. You are too modest about your own charms. Would anybody put up a parasol to keep off the soothing autumn moonlight?

Shakuntala (*smiling*). I suppose I shall have to obey orders. (*She meditates.*)

King. It is only natural that I should forget to wink when I see my darling. For

One clinging eyebrow lifted,
  As fitting words she seeks,
Her face reveals her passion
  For me in glowing cheeks.

Shakuntala. Well, I have thought out a little song. But I haven't anything to write with.

Priyamvada. Here is a lotus-leaf, glossy as a parrot's breast. You can cut the letters in it with your nails.

Shakuntala. Now listen, and tell me whether it makes sense.

The two friends. Please.

Shakuntala (*reads*).

I know not if I read your heart aright;
  Why, pitiless, do you distress me so?
I only know that longing day and night
  Tosses my restless body to and fro,
  That yearns for you, the source of all its woe.

King (*advancing*).

Though Love torments you, slender maid,
  Yet he consumes me quite,
As daylight shuts night-blooming flowers
  And slays the moon outright.

The two friends (*perceive the king and rise joyfully*). Welcome to the wish that is fulfilled without delay. (SHAKUNTALA *tries to rise.*)

King. Do not try to rise, beautiful Shakuntala.

Your limbs from which the strength is fled,
That crush the blossoms of your bed
And bruise the lotus-leaves, may be
Pardoned a breach of courtesy.

Shakuntala (*sadly to herself*). Oh, my heart, you were so impatient, and now you find no answer to make.

Anusuya. Your Majesty, pray do this stone bench the honour of sitting upon it. (SHAKUNTALA *edges away*.)

King (*seating himself*). Priyamvada, I trust your friend's illness is not dangerous.

Priyamvada (*smiling*). A remedy is being applied and it will soon be better. It is plain, sir, that you and she love each other. But I love her too, and I must say something over again.

King. Pray do not hesitate. It always causes pain in the end, to leave unsaid what one longs to say.

Priyamvada. Then listen, sir.

King. I am all attention.

Priyamvada. It is the king's duty to save hermit-folk from all suffering. Is not that good Scripture?

King. There is no text more urgent.

Priyamvada. Well, our friend has been brought to this sad state by her love for you. Will you not take pity on her and save her life?

King. We cherish the same desire. I feel it a great honour.

Shakuntala (*with a jealous smile*). Oh, don't detain the good king. He is separated from the court ladies, and he is anxious to go back to them.

King. Bewitching eyes that found my heart,
You surely see
It could no longer live apart,
Nor faithless be.
I bear Love's arrows as I can;
Wound not with doubt a wounded man.

Anusuya. But, your Majesty, we hear that kings have many favourites. You must act in such a way that our friend may not become a cause of grief to her family.

King. What more can I say?

Though many queens divide my court,
But two support the throne;
Your friend will find a rival in
The sea-girt earth alone.

The two friends. We are content. (SHAKUNTALA *betrays her joy*.)

Priyamvada (*aside to* ANUSUYA). Look, Anusuya! See how the dear girl's life is coming back moment by moment—just like a peahen in summer when the first rainy breezes come.

Shakuntala. You must please ask the king's pardon for the rude things we said when we were talking together.

The two friends (*smiling*). Anybody who says it was rude, may ask his pardon. Nobody else feels guilty.

Shakuntala. Your Majesty, pray forgive what we said when we did not know that you were present. I am afraid that we say a great many things behind a person's back.

King (*smiling*).

Your fault is pardoned if I may
  Relieve my weariness
By sitting on the flower-strewn couch
  Your fevered members press.

Priyamvada. But that will not be enough to satisfy him.

Shakuntala (*feigning anger*). Stop! You are a rude girl. You make fun of me when I am in this condition.

Anusuya (*looking out of the arbour*). Priyamvada, there is a little fawn, looking all about him. He has probably lost his mother and is trying to find her. I am going to help him.

Priyamvada. He is a frisky little fellow. You can't catch him alone. I'll go with you. (*They start to go.*)

Shakuntala. I will not let you go and leave me alone.

The two friends (*smiling*). You alone, when the king of the world is with you! (*Exeunt.*)

Shakuntala. Are my friends gone?

King (*looking about*). Do not be anxious, beautiful Shakuntala. Have you not a humble servant here, to take the place of your friends? Then tell me:

Shall I employ the moistened lotus-leaf
To fan away your weariness and grief?
Or take your lily feet upon my knee
And rub them till you rest more easily?

Shakuntala. I will not offend against those to whom I owe honour. (*She rises weakly and starts to walk away.*)

King (*detaining her*). The day is still hot, beautiful Shakuntala, and you are feverish.

Leave not the blossom-dotted couch
To wander in the midday heat,
With lotus-petals on your breast,
With fevered limbs and stumbling feet.

(*He lays his hand upon her.*)

Shakuntala. Oh, don't! Don't! For I am not mistress of myself. Yet what can I do now? I had no one to help me but my friends.

King. I am rebuked.

Shakuntala. I was not thinking of your Majesty. I was accusing fate.

King. Why accuse a fate that brings what you desire?

Shakuntala. Why not accuse a fate that robs me of self-control and tempts me with the virtues of another?

King (*to himself*).

Though deeply longing, maids are coy
And bid their wooers wait;
Though eager for united joy
In love, they hesitate.

Love cannot torture them, nor move
Their hearts to sudden mating;
Perhaps they even torture love
By their procrastinating.

(SHAKUNTALA *moves away.*)

King. Why should I not have my way? (*He approaches and seizes her dress.*)

Shakuntala. Oh, sir! Be a gentleman. There are hermits wandering about.

King. Do not fear your family, beautiful Shakuntala. Father Kanva knows the holy law. He will not regret it.

For many a hermit maiden who
By simple, voluntary rite
Dispensed with priest and witness, yet
Found favour in her father's sight.

(*He looks about.*) Ah, I have come into the open air. (*He leaves* SHAKUNTALA *and retraces his steps.*)

Shakuntala (*takes a step, then turns with an eager gesture*). O King, I cannot do as you would have me. You hardly know me after this short talk. But oh, do not forget me.

King.

When evening comes, the shadow of the tree
Is cast far forward, yet does not depart;
Even so, belovèd, wheresoe'er you be,
The thought of you can never leave my heart.

Shakuntala (*takes a few steps. To herself*). Oh, oh! When I hear him speak so, my feet will not move away. I will hide in this amaranth hedge and see how long his love lasts. (*She hides and waits.*)

King. Oh, my belovèd, my love for you is my whole life, yet you leave me and go away without a thought.

Your body, soft as siris-flowers,
Engages passion's utmost powers;
How comes it that your heart is hard
As stalks that siris-blossoms guard?

Shakuntala. When I hear this, I have no power to go.

King. What have I to do here, where she is not? (*He gazes on the ground.*) Ah, I cannot go.

The perfumed lotus-chain
That once was worn by her
Fetters and keeps my heart
A hopeless prisoner. (*He lifts it reverently.*)

Shakuntala (*looking at her arm*). Why, I was so weak and ill that when the lotus-bracelet fell off, I did not even notice it.

King (*laying the lotus-bracelet on his heart*). Ah!

Once, dear, on your sweet arm it lay,
And on my heart shall ever stay;
Though you disdain to give me joy,
I find it in a lifeless toy.

Shakuntala. I cannot hold back after that. I will use the bracelet as an excuse for my coming. (*She approaches.*)

King (*seeing her. Joyfully*). The queen of my life! As soon as I complained, fate proved kind to me.

No sooner did the thirsty bird
  With parching throat complain,
Than forming clouds in heaven stirred
  And sent the streaming rain.

Shakuntala (*standing before the king*). When I was going away, sir, I remembered that this lotus-bracelet had fallen from my arm, and I have come back for it. My heart seemed to tell me that you had taken it. Please give it back, or you will betray me, and yourself too, to the hermits.

King. I will restore it on one condition.

Shakuntala. What condition?

King. That I may myself place it where it belongs.

Shakuntala (*to herself*). What can I do? (*She approaches.*)

King. Let us sit on this stone bench. (*They walk to the bench and sit down.*)

King (*taking* SHAKUNTALA'S *hand*). Ah!

When Shiva's anger burned the tree
  Of love in quenchless fire,
Did heavenly fate preserve a shoot
  To deck my heart's desire?

Shakuntala (*feeling his touch*). Hasten, my dear, hasten.

King (*joyfully to himself*). Now I am content. She speaks as a wife to her husband. (*Aloud.*) Beautiful Shakuntala, the clasp of the bracelet is not very firm. May I fasten it in another way?

Shakuntala (*smiling*). If you like.

King (*artfully delaying before he fastens it*). See, my beautiful girl!

The lotus-chain is dazzling white
As is the slender moon at night.
Perhaps it was the moon on high
That joined her horns and left the sky,
Believing that your lovely arm
Would, more than heaven, enhance her charm.

Shakuntala. I cannot see it. The pollen from the lotus over my ear has blown into my eye.

King (*smiling*). Will you permit me to blow it away?

Shakuntala. I should not like to be an object of pity. But why should I not trust you?

King. Do not have such thoughts. A new servant does not transgress orders.

Shakuntala. It is this exaggerated courtesy that frightens me.

King (*to himself*). I shall not break the bonds of this sweet servitude. (*He starts to raise her face to his.* SHAKUNTALA *resists a little, then is passive.*)

King. Oh, my bewitching girl, have no fear of me. (SHAKUNTALA *darts a glance at him, then looks down. The king raises her face. Aside.*)

Her sweetly trembling lip
With virgin invitation
Provokes my soul to sip
Delighted fascination.

Shakuntala. You seem slow, dear, in fulfilling your promise.

King. The lotus over your ear is so near your eye, and so like it, that I was confused. (*He gently blows her eye.*)

Shakuntala. Thank you. I can see quite well now. But I am ashamed not to make any return for your kindness.

King. What more could I ask?

It ought to be enough for me
To hover round your fragrant face;
Is not the lotus-haunting bee
Content with perfume and with grace?

Shakuntala. But what does he do if he is not content?

King. This! This! (*He draws her face to his.*)

A voice behind the scenes. O sheldrake bride, bid your mate farewell. The night is come.

Shakuntala (*listening excitedly*). Oh, my dear, this is Mother Gautami, come to inquire about me. Please hide among the branches. (*The king conceals himself. Enter* GAUTAMI, *with a bowl in her hand.*)

Gautami. Here is the holy water, my child. (*She sees* SHAKUNTALA *and helps her to rise.*) So ill, and all alone here with the gods?

Shakuntala. It was just a moment ago that Priyamvada and Anusuya went down to the river.

Gautami (*sprinkling* SHAKUNTALA *with the holy water*). May you live long and happy, my child. Has the fever gone down? (*She touches her.*)

Shakuntala. There is a difference, mother.

Gautami. The sun is setting. Come, let us go to the cottage.

Shakuntala (*weakly rising. To herself*). Oh, my heart, you delayed when your desire came of itself. Now see what you have done. (*She takes a step, then turns around. Aloud.*) O bower that took away my pain, I bid you farewell until another blissful hour. (*Exeunt* SHAKUNTALA *and* GAUTAMI.)

King (*advancing with a sigh.*) The path to happiness is strewn with obstacles.

Her face, adorned with soft eye-lashes,
Adorable with trembling flashes
Of half-denial, in memory lingers;
The sweet lips guarded by her fingers,
The head that drooped upon her shoulder—
Why was I not a little bolder?

Where shall I go now? Let me stay a moment in this bower where my belovèd lay. (*He looks about.*)

The flower-strewn bed whereon her body tossed;
The bracelet, fallen from her arm and lost;
The dear love-missive, in the lotus-leaf
Cut by her nails: assuage my absent grief
And occupy my eyes—I have no power,
Though she is gone, to leave the reedy bower.

(*He reflects.*) Alas! I did wrong to delay when I had found my love. So now

If she will grant me but one other meeting,
I'll not delay; for happiness is fleeting;
So plans my foolish, self-defeated heart;
But when she comes, I play the coward's part.

A voice behind the scenes. O King!

The flames rise heavenward from the evening altar;
  And round the sacrifices, blazing high,
Flesh-eating demons stalk, like red cloud-masses,
  And cast colossal shadows on the sky.

King (*listens. Resolutely*). Have no fear, hermits. I am here. (*Exit.*)

ACT IV

Shakuntala's Departure

Scene I

(*Enter the two friends, gathering flowers.*)

Anusuya. Priyamvada, dear Shakuntala has been properly married by the voluntary ceremony and she has a husband worthy of her. And yet I am not quite satisfied.

Priyamvada. Why not?

Anusuya. The sacrifice is over and the good king was dismissed to-day by the hermits. He has gone back to the city and there he is surrounded by hundreds of court ladies. I wonder whether he will remember poor Shakuntala or not.

Priyamvada. You need not be anxious about that. Such handsome men are sure to be good. But there is something else to think about. I don't know what Father will have to say when he comes back from his pilgrimage and hears about it.

Anusuya. I believe that he will be pleased.

Priyamvada. Why?

Anusuya. Why not? You know he wanted to give his daughter to a lover worthy of her. If fate brings this about of itself, why shouldn't Father be happy?

Priyamvada. I suppose you are right. (*She looks at her flower-basket.*) My dear, we have gathered flowers enough for the sacrifice.

Anusuya. But we must make an offering to the gods that watch over Shakuntala's marriage. We had better gather more.

Priyamvada. Very well. (*They do so.*)

A voice behind the scenes. Who will bid me welcome?

Anusuya (*listening*). My dear, it sounds like a guest announcing himself.

Priyamvada. Well, Shakuntala is near the cottage. (*Reflecting.*) Ah, but to-day her heart is far away. Come, we must do with the flowers we have. (*They start to walk away.*)

The voice. Do you dare despise a guest like me?

Because your heart, by loving fancies blinded,
Has scorned a guest in pious life grown old,
Your lover shall forget you though reminded,
Or think of you as of a story told.

(*The two girls listen and show dejection.*)

Priyamvada. Oh, dear! The very thing has happened. The dear, absent-minded girl has offended some worthy man.

Anusuya (*looking ahead*). My dear, this is no ordinary somebody. It is the great sage Durvasas, the irascible. See how he strides away!

Priyamvada. Nothing burns like fire. Run, fall at his feet, bring him back, while I am getting water to wash his feet.

Anusuya. I will. (*Exit.*)

Priyamvada (*stumbling*). There! I stumbled in my excitement, and the flower-basket fell out of my hand. (*She collects the scattered flowers.* ANUSUYA *returns.*)

Anusuya. My dear, he is anger incarnate. Who could appease him? But I softened him a little.

Priyamvada. Even that is a good deal for him. Tell me about it.

Anusuya. When he would not turn back, I fell at his feet and prayed to him. "Holy sir," I said, "remember her former devotion and pardon this offence. Your daughter did not recognise your great and holy power to-day."

Priyamvada. And then——

Anusuya. Then he said: "My words must be fulfilled. But the curse shall be lifted when her lover sees a gem which he has given her for a token." And so he vanished.

Priyamvada. We can breathe again. When the good king went away, he put a ring, engraved with his own name, on Shakuntala's finger to remember him by. That will save her.

Anusuya. Come, we must finish the sacrifice for her. (*They walk about.*)

Priyamvada (*gazing*). Just look, Anusuya! There is the dear girl, with her cheek resting on her left hand. She looks like a painted picture. She is thinking about him. How could she notice a guest when she has forgotten herself?

Anusuya. Priyamvada, we two must keep this thing to ourselves. We must be careful of the dear girl. You know how delicate she is.

Priyamvada. Would any one sprinkle a jasmine-vine with scalding water? (*Exeunt ambo.*)

SCENE II.—*Early Morning*

(*Enter a pupil of* KANVA, *just risen from sleep.*)

Pupil. Father Kanva has returned from his pilgrimage, and has bidden me find out what time it is. I will go into the open air and see how much of the night remains. (*He walks and looks about.*) See! The dawn is breaking. For already

The moon behind the western mount is sinking;
The eastern sun is heralded by dawn;
From heaven's twin lights, their fall and glory linking,
Brave lessons of submission may be drawn.

And again:

Night-blooming lilies, when the moon is hidden,
Have naught but memories of beauty left.
Hard, hard to bear! Her lot whom heaven has bidden
To live alone, of love and lover reft.

And again:

On jujube-trees the blushing dewdrops falter;
The peacock wakes and leaves the cottage thatch;
A deer is rising near the hoof-marked altar,
And stretching, stands, the day's new life to catch.

And yet again:

The moon that topped the loftiest mountain ranges,
That slew the darkness in the midmost sky,
Is fallen from heaven, and all her glory changes:
So high to rise, so low at last to lie!

Anusuya (*entering hurriedly. To herself*). That is just what happens to the innocent. Shakuntala has been treated shamefully by the king.

Pupil. I will tell Father Kanva that the hour of morning sacrifice is come. (*Exit.*)

Anusuya. The dawn is breaking. I am awake bright and early. But what shall I do now that I am awake? My hands refuse to attend to the ordinary morning tasks. Well, let love take its course. For the dear, pure-minded girl trusted him—the traitor! Perhaps it is not the good king's fault. It must be the curse of Durvasas. Otherwise, how could the good king say such beautiful things, and then let all this time pass without even sending a message? (*She reflects.*) Yes, we must send him the ring he left as a token. But whom shall we ask to take it? The hermits are unsympathetic because they have never suffered. It seemed as if her friends were to blame and so, try as we might, we could not tell Father Kanva that Shakuntala was married to Dushyanta and was expecting a baby. Oh, what shall we do? (*Enter* PRIYAMVADA.)

Priyamvada. Hurry, Anusuya, hurry! We are getting Shakuntala ready for her journey.

Anusuya (*astonished*). What do you mean, my dear?

Priyamvada. Listen. I just went to Shakuntala, to ask if she had slept well.

Anusuya. And then——

Priyamvada. I found her hiding her face for shame, and Father Kanva was embracing her and encouraging her. "My child," he said, "I bring you joy. The offering fell straight in the sacred fire, and auspicious smoke rose toward the sacrificer. My pains for you have proved like instruction given to a good student; they have brought me no regret. This very day I shall give you an escort of hermits and send you to your husband."

Anusuya. But, my dear, who told Father Kanva about it?

Priyamvada. A voice from heaven that recited a verse when he had entered the fire-sanctuary.

Anusuya (*astonished*). What did it say?

Priyamvada. Listen. (*Speaking in good Sanskrit.*)

Know, Brahman, that your child,
  Like the fire-pregnant tree,
Bears kingly seed that shall be born
  For earth's prosperity.

Anusuya (*hugging* PRIYAMVADA). I am so glad, dear. But my joy is half sorrow when I think that Shakuntala is going to be taken away this very day.

Priyamvada. We must hide our sorrow as best we can. The poor girl must be made happy to-day.

Anusuya. Well, here is a cocoa-nut casket, hanging on a branch of the mango-tree. I put flower-pollen in it for this very purpose. It keeps fresh, you know. Now you wrap it in a lotus-leaf, and I will get yellow pigment and earth from a sacred spot and blades of panic grass for the happy ceremony. (PRIYAMVADA *does so. Exit* ANUSUYA.)

A voice behind the scenes. Gautami, bid the worthy Sharngarava and Sharadvata make ready to escort my daughter Shakuntala.

Priyamvada (*listening*). Hurry, Anusuya, hurry! They are calling the hermits who are going to Hastinapura. (*Enter* ANUSUYA, *with materials for the ceremony*.)

Anusuya. Come, dear, let us go. (*They walk about*.)

Priyamvada (*looking ahead*). There is Shakuntala. She took the ceremonial bath at sunrise, and now the hermit-women are giving her rice-cakes and wishing her happiness. Let's go to her. (*They do so. Enter* SHAKUNTALA *with attendants as described, and* GAUTAMI.)

Shakuntala. Holy women, I salute you.

Gautami. My child, may you receive the happy title "queen," showing that your husband honours you.

Hermit-women. My dear, may you become the mother of a hero. (*Exeunt all but* GAUTAMI.)

The two friends (*approaching*). Did you have a good bath, dear?

Shakuntala. Good morning, girls. Sit here.

The two friends (*seating themselves*). Now stand straight, while we go through the happy ceremony.

Shakuntala. It has happened often enough, but I ought to be very grateful to-day. Shall I ever be adorned by my friends again? (*She weeps*.)

The two friends. You ought not to weep, dear, at this happy time. (*They wipe the tears away and adorn her*.)

Priyamvada. You are so beautiful, you ought to have the finest gems. It seems like an insult to give you these hermitage things. (*Enter* HARITA, *a hermit-youth, with ornaments*.)

Harita. Here are ornaments for our lady. (*The women look at them in astonishment.*)

Gautami. Harita, my son, whence come these things?

Harita. From the holy power of Father Kanva.

Gautami. A creation of his mind?

Harita. Not quite. Listen. Father Kanva sent us to gather blossoms from the trees for Shakuntala, and then

One tree bore fruit, a silken marriage dress
That shamed the moon in its white loveliness;
Another gave us lac-dye for the feet;
From others, fairy hands extended, sweet
Like flowering twigs, as far as to the wrist,
And gave us gems, to adorn her as we list.

Priyamvada (*looking at* SHAKUNTALA). A bee may be born in a hole in a tree, but she likes the honey of the lotus.

Gautami. This gracious favour is a token of the queenly happiness which you are to enjoy in your husband's palace. (SHAKUNTALA *shows embarrassment.*)

Harita. Father Kanva has gone to the bank of the Malini, to perform his ablutions. I will tell him of the favour shown us by the trees. (*Exit.*)

Anusuya. My dear, we poor girls never saw such ornaments. How shall we adorn you? (*She stops to think, and to look at the ornaments.*) But we have seen pictures. Perhaps we can arrange them right.

Shakuntala. I know how clever you are. (*The two friends adorn her. Enter* KANVA, *returning after his ablutions.*)

Kanva.

Shakuntala must go to-day;
I miss her now at heart;
I dare not speak a loving word
Or choking tears will start.

My eyes are dim with anxious thought;
Love strikes me to the life:
And yet I strove for pious peace—
I have no child, no wife.

What must a father feel, when come
The pangs of parting from his child at home?

(*He walks about.*)

The two friends. There, Shakuntala, we have arranged your ornaments. Now put on this beautiful silk dress. (SHAKUNTALA *rises and does so.*)

Gautami. My child, here is your father. The eyes with which he seems to embrace you are overflowing with tears of joy. You must greet him properly. (SHAKUNTALA *makes a shamefaced reverence.*)

Kanva. My child,

Like Sharmishtha, Yayati's wife,
  Win favour measured by your worth;
And may you bear a kingly son
  Like Puru, who shall rule the earth.

Gautami. My child, this is not a prayer, but a benediction.

Kanva. My daughter, walk from left to right about the fires in which the offering has just been thrown. (*All walk about.*)

The holy fires around the altar kindle,
  And at their margins sacred grass is piled;
Beneath their sacrificial odours dwindle
  Misfortunes. May the fires protect you, child!

(SHAKUNTALA *walks about them from left to right.*)

Kanva. Now you may start, my daughter. (*He glances about.*) Where are Sharngarava and Sharadvata? (*Enter the two pupils.*)

The two pupils. We are here, Father.

Kanva. Sharngarava, my son, lead the way for your sister.

Sharngarava. Follow me. (*They all walk about.*)

Kanva. O trees of the pious grove, in which the fairies dwell,

She would not drink till she had wet
  Your roots, a sister's duty,
Nor pluck your flowers; she loves you yet
  Far more than selfish beauty.

'Twas festival in her pure life
  When budding blossoms showed;
And now she leaves you as a wife—
  Oh, speed her on her road!

Sharngarava (*listening to the song of koïl-birds*). Father,

The trees are answering your prayer
In cooing cuckoo-song,
Bidding Shakuntala farewell,
Their sister for so long.

Invisible beings.

May lily-dotted lakes delight your eye;
May shade-trees bid the heat of noonday cease;
May soft winds blow the lotus-pollen nigh;
May all your path be pleasantness and peace.

(*All listen in astonishment.*)

Gautami. My child, the fairies of the pious grove bid you farewell. For they love the household. Pay reverence to the holy ones.

Shakuntala (*does so. Aside to* PRIYAMVADA). Priyamvada, I long to see my husband, and yet my feet will hardly move. It is hard, hard to leave the hermitage.

Priyamvada. You are not the only one to feel sad at this farewell. See how the whole grove feels at parting from you.

The grass drops from the feeding doe;
The peahen stops her dance;
Pale, trembling leaves are falling slow,
The tears of clinging plants.

Shakuntala (*recalling something*). Father, I must say good-bye to the spring-creeper, my sister among the vines.

Kanva. I know your love for her. See! Here she is at your right hand.

Shakuntala (*approaches the vine and embraces it*). Vine sister, embrace me too with your arms, these branches. I shall be far away from you after to-day. Father, you must care for her as you did for me.

Kanva. My child, you found the lover who
Had long been sought by me;
No longer need I watch for you;
I'll give the vine a lover true,
This handsome mango-tree.

And now start on your journey.

Shakuntala (*going to the two friends*). Dear girls, I leave her in your care too.

The two friends. But who will care for poor us? (*They shed tears.*)

Kanva. Anusuya! Priyamvada! Do not weep. It is you who should cheer Shakuntala. (*All walk about.*)

Shakuntala. Father, there is the pregnant doe, wandering about near the cottage. When she becomes a happy mother, you must send some one to bring me the good news. Do not forget.

Kanva. I shall not forget, my child.

Shakuntala (*stumbling*). Oh, oh! Who is it that keeps pulling at my dress, as if to hinder me? (*She turns round to see.*)

Kanva. It is the fawn whose lip, when torn
By kusha-grass, you soothed with oil;
The fawn who gladly nibbled corn
Held in your hand; with loving toil
You have adopted him, and he
Would never leave you willingly.

Shakuntala. My dear, why should you follow me when I am going away from home? Your mother died when you were born and I brought you up. Now I am leaving you, and Father Kanva will take care of you. Go back, dear! Go back! (*She walks away, weeping.*)

Kanva. Do not weep, my child. Be brave. Look at the path before you.

Be brave, and check the rising tears
That dim your lovely eyes;
Your feet are stumbling on the path
That so uneven lies.

Sharngarava. Holy Father, the Scripture declares that one should accompany a departing loved one only to the first water. Pray give us your commands on the bank of this pond, and then return.

Kanva. Then let us rest in the shade of this fig-tree. (*All do so.*) What commands would it be fitting for me to lay on King Dushyanta? (*He reflects.*)

Anusuya. My dear, there is not a living thing in the whole hermitage that is not grieving to-day at saying good-bye to you. Look!

The sheldrake does not heed his mate
  Who calls behind the lotus-leaf;
He drops the lily from his bill
  And turns on you a glance of grief.

Kanva. Son Sharngarava, when you present Shakuntala to the king, give him this message from me.

Remembering my religious worth,
Your own high race, the love poured forth
By her, forgetful of her friends,
Pay her what honour custom lends
To all your wives. And what fate gives
Beyond, will please her relatives.

Sharngarava. I will not forget your message, Father.

Kanva (*turning to* SHAKUNTALA). My child, I must now give you my counsel. Though I live in the forest, I have some knowledge of the world.

Sharngarava. True wisdom, Father, gives insight into everything.

Kanva. My child, when you have entered your husband's home,

Obey your elders; and be very kind
To rivals; never be perversely blind
And angry with your husband, even though he
Should prove less faithful than a man might be;
Be as courteous to servants as you may,
Not puffed with pride in this your happy day:
Thus does a maiden grow into a wife;
But self-willed women are the curse of life.

But what does Gautami say?

Gautami. This is advice sufficient for a bride. (*To* SHAKUNTALA.) You will not forget, my child.

Kanva. Come, my daughter, embrace me and your friends.

Shakuntala. Oh, Father! Must my friends turn back too?

Kanva. My daughter, they too must some day be given in marriage. Therefore they may not go to court. Gautami will go with you.

Shakuntala (*throwing her arms about her father*). I am torn from my father's breast like a vine stripped from a sandal-tree on the Malabar hills. How can I live in another soil? (*She weeps.*)

Kanva. My daughter, why distress yourself so?

> A noble husband's honourable wife,
> You are to spend a busy, useful life
> In the world's eye; and soon, as eastern skies
> Bring forth the sun, from you there shall arise
> A child, a blessing and a comfort strong—
> You will not miss me, dearest daughter, long.

Shakuntala (*falling at his feet*). Farewell, Father.

Kanva. My daughter, may all that come to you which I desire for you.

Shakuntala (*going to her two friends*). Come, girls! Embrace me, both of you together.

The two friends (*do so*). Dear, if the good king should perhaps be slow to recognise you, show him the ring with his own name engraved on it.

Shakuntala. Your doubts make my heart beat faster.

The two friends. Do not be afraid, dear. Love is timid.

Sharngarava (*looking about*). Father, the sun is in mid-heaven. She must hasten.

Shakuntala (*embracing* KANVA *once more*). Father, when shall I see the pious grove again?

Kanva. My daughter,

> When you have shared for many years
> The king's thoughts with the earth,
> When to a son who knows no fears
> You shall have given birth,
>
> When, trusted to the son you love,
> Your royal labours cease,
> Come with your husband to the grove
> And end your days in peace.

Gautami. My child, the hour of your departure is slipping by. Bid your father turn back. No, she would never do that. Pray turn back, sir.

Kanva. Child, you interrupt my duties in the pious grove.

Shakuntala. Yes, Father. You will be busy in the grove. You will not miss me. But oh! I miss you.

Kanva. How can you think me so indifferent? (*He sighs.*)

My lonely sorrow will not go,
For seeds you scattered here
Before the cottage door, will grow;
And I shall see them, dear.

Go. And peace go with you. (*Exit* SHAKUNTALA, *with* GAUTAMI, SHARNGARAVA, *and* SHARADVATA.)

The two friends (*gazing long after her. Mournfully*). Oh, oh! Shakuntala is lost among the trees.

Kanva. Anusuya! Priyamvada! Your companion is gone. Choke down your grief and follow me. (*They start to go back.*)

The two friends. Father, the grove seems empty without Shakuntala.

Kanva. So love interprets. (*He walks about, sunk in thought.*) Ah! I have sent Shakuntala away, and now I am myself again. For

A girl is held in trust, another's treasure;
To arms of love my child to-day is given;
And now I feel a calm and sacred pleasure;
I have restored the pledge that came from heaven.

(*Exeunt omnes.*)

ACT V

Shakuntala's Rejection

(*Enter a chamberlain.*)

Chamberlain (*sighing*). Alas! To what a state am I reduced!

I once assumed the staff of reed
 For custom's sake alone,
As officer to guard at need
 The ladies round the throne.
But years have passed away and made
It serve, my tottering steps to aid.

The king is within. I will tell him of the urgent business which demands his attention. (*He takes a few steps.*) But what is the business? (*He recalls it.*) Yes, I remember. Certain hermits, pupils of Kanva, desire to see his Majesty. Strange, strange!

The mind of age is like a lamp
 Whose oil is running thin;
One moment it is shining bright,
 Then darkness closes in.

(*He walks and looks about.*) Here is his Majesty.

He does not seek—until a father's care
 Is shown his subjects—rest in solitude;
As a great elephant recks not of the sun
 Until his herd is sheltered in the wood.

In truth, I hesitate to announce the coming of Kanva's pupils to the king. For he has this moment risen from the throne of justice. But kings are never weary. For

The sun unyokes his horses never;
 Blows night and day the breeze;
Shesha upholds the world forever:
 And kings are like to these.

(*He walks about. Enter the king, the clown, and retinue according to rank.*)

King (*betraying the cares of office*). Every one is happy on attaining his desire—except a king. His difficulties increase with his power. Thus:

Security slays nothing but ambition;
With great possessions, troubles gather thick;
Pain grows, not lessens, with a king's position,
As when one's hand must hold the sunshade's stick.

Two court poets behind the scenes. Victory to your Majesty.

First poet.

The world you daily guard and bless,
Not heeding pain or weariness;
Thus is your nature made.
A tree will brave the noonday, when
The sun is fierce, that weary men
May rest beneath its shade.

Second poet.

Vice bows before the royal rod;
Strife ceases at your kingly nod;
You are our strong defender.
Friends come to all whose wealth is sure,
But you, alike to rich and poor,
Are friend both strong and tender.

King (*listening*). Strange! I was wearied by the demands of my office, but this renews my spirit.

Clown. Does a bull forget that he is tired when you call him the leader of the herd?

King (*smiling*). Well, let us sit down. (*They seat themselves, and the retinue arranges itself. A lute is heard behind the scenes.*)

Clown (*listening*). My friend, listen to what is going on in the music-room. Some one is playing a lute, and keeping good time. I suppose Lady Hansavati is practising.

King. Be quiet. I wish to listen.

Chamberlain (*looks at the king*). Ah, the king is occupied. I must await his leisure. (*He stands aside.*)

A song behind the scenes.

You who kissed the mango-flower,
Honey-loving bee,
Gave her all your passion's power,
Ah, so tenderly!

How can you be tempted so
By the lily, pet?
Fresher honey 's sweet, I know;
But can you forget?

King. What an entrancing song!

Clown. But, man, don't you understand what the words mean?

King (*smiling*). I was once devoted to Queen Hansavati. And the rebuke comes from her. Friend Madhavya, tell Queen Hansavati in my name that the rebuke is a very pretty one.

Clown. Yes, sir. (*He rises.*) But, man, you are using another fellow's fingers to grab a bear's tail-feathers with. I have about as much chance of salvation as a monk who hasn't forgotten his passions.

King. Go. Soothe her like a gentleman.

Clown. I suppose I must. (*Exit.*)

King (*to himself*). Why am I filled with wistfulness on hearing such a song? I am not separated from one I love. And yet

In face of sweet presentment
Or harmonies of sound,
Man e'er forgets contentment,
By wistful longings bound.

There must be recollections
Of things not seen on earth,
Deep nature's predilections,
Loves earlier than birth.

(*He shows the wistfulness that comes from unremembered things.*)

Chamberlain (*approaching*). Victory to your Majesty. Here are hermits who dwell in the forest at the foot of the Himalayas. They bring women with them, and they carry a message from Kanva. What is your pleasure with regard to them?

King (*astonished*). Hermits? Accompanied by women? From Kanva?

Chamberlain. Yes.

King. Request my chaplain Somarata in my name to

receive these hermits in the manner prescribed by Scripture, and to conduct them himself before me. I will await them in a place fit for their reception.

Chamberlain. Yes, your Majesty. (*Exit.*)

King (*rising*). Vetravati, conduct me to the fire-sanctuary.

Portress. Follow me, your Majesty. (*She walks about.*) Your Majesty, here is the terrace of the fire-sanctuary. It is beautiful, for it has just been swept, and near at hand is the cow that yields the milk of sacrifice. Pray ascend it.

King (*ascends and stands leaning on the shoulder of an attendant.*) Vetravati, with what purpose does Father Kanva send these hermits to me?

Do leaguèd powers of sin conspire
To balk religion's pure desire?
Has wrong been done to beasts that roam
Contented round the hermits' home?
Do plants no longer bud and flower,
To warn me of abuse of power?
These doubts and more assail my mind,
But leave me puzzled, lost, and blind.

Portress. How could these things be in a hermitage that rests in the fame of the king's arm? No, I imagine they have come to pay homage to their king, and to congratulate him on his pious rule.

(*Enter the chaplain and the chamberlain, conducting the two pupils of* KANVA, *with* GAUTAMI *and* SHAKUNTALA.)

Chamberlain. Follow me, if you please.

Sharngarava. Friend Sharadvata,

The king is noble and to virtue true;
None dwelling here commit the deed of shame;
Yet we ascetics view the worldly crew
As in a house all lapped about with flame.

Sharadvata. Sharngarava, your emotion on entering the city is quite just. As for me,

Free from the world and all its ways,
I see them spending worldly days
As clean men view men smeared with oil,
As pure men, those whom passions soil,
As waking men view men asleep,
As free men, those in bondage deep.

Chaplain. That is why men like you are great.

Shakuntala (*observing an evil omen*). Oh, why does my right eye throb?

Gautami. Heaven avert the omen, my child. May happiness wait upon you. (*They walk about.*)

Chaplain (*indicating the king*). O hermits, here is he who protects those of every station and of every age. He has already risen, and awaits you. Behold him.

Sharngarava. Yes, it is admirable, but not surprising. For

Fruit-laden trees bend down to earth;
  The water-pregnant clouds hang low;
Good men are not puffed up by power—
  The unselfish are by nature so.

Portress. Your Majesty, the hermits seem to be happy. They give you gracious looks.

King (*observing* SHAKUNTALA). Ah!

Who is she, shrouded in the veil
  That dims her beauty's lustre,
Among the hermits like a flower
  Round which the dead leaves cluster?

Portress. Your Majesty, she is well worth looking at.

King. Enough! I must not gaze upon another's wife.

Shakuntala (*laying her hand on her breast. Aside*). Oh, my heart, why tremble so? Remember his constant love and be brave.

Chaplain (*advancing*). Hail, your Majesty. The hermits have been received as Scripture enjoins. They have a message from their teacher. May you be pleased to hear it.

King (*respectfully*). I am all attention.

The two pupils (*raising their right hands*). Victory, O King.

King (*bowing low*). I salute you all.

The two pupils. All hail.

King. Does your pious life proceed without disturbance?

The two pupils.

How could the pious duties fail
  While you defend the right?
Or how could darkness' power prevail
  O'er sunbeams shining bright?

King (*to himself*). Indeed, my royal title is no empty one. (*Aloud.*) Is holy Kanva in health?

Sharngarava. O King, those who have religious power can command health. He asks after your welfare and sends this message.

King. What are his commands?

Sharngarava. He says: "Since you have met this my daughter and have married her, I give you my glad consent. For

You are the best of worthy men, they say;
  And she, I know, Good Works personified;
The Creator wrought for ever and a day,
  In wedding such a virtuous groom and bride.

She is with child. Take her and live with her in virtue."

Gautami. Bless you, sir. I should like to say that no one invites me to speak.

King. Speak, mother.

Gautami.

Did she with father speak or mother?
  Did you engage her friends in speech?
Your faith was plighted each to other;
  Let each be faithful now to each.

Shakuntala. What will my husband say?

King (*listening with anxious suspicion*). What is this insinuation?

Shakuntala (*to herself*). Oh, oh! So haughty and so slanderous!

Sharngarava. "What is this insinuation?" What is your question? Surely you know the world's ways well enough.

Because the world suspects a wife
  Who does not share her husband's lot,
Her kinsmen wish her to abide
  With him, although he love her not.

King. You cannot mean that this young woman is my wife.

Shakuntala (*sadly to herself*). Oh, my heart, you feared it, and now it has come.

Sharngarava. O King,

A king, and shrink when love is done,
Turn coward's back on truth, and flee!

King. What means this dreadful accusation?

Sharngarava (furiously).

O drunk with power! We might have known
That you were steeped in treachery.

King. A stinging rebuke!

Gautami (to SHAKUNTALA*).* Forget your shame, my child. I will remove your veil. Then your husband will recognise you. *(She does so.)*

King (observing SHAKUNTALA. *To himself).*

As my heart ponders whether I could ever
Have wed this woman that has come to me
In tortured loveliness, as I endeavour
To bring it back to mind, then like a bee

That hovers round a jasmine flower at dawn,
While frosty dews of morning still o'erweave it,
And hesitates to sip ere they be gone,
I cannot taste the sweet, and cannot leave it.

Portress (to herself). What a virtuous king he is! Would any other man hesitate when he saw such a pearl of a woman coming of her own accord?

Sharngarava. Have you nothing to say, O King?

King. Hermit, I have taken thought. I cannot believe that this woman is my wife. She is plainly with child. How can I take her, confessing myself an adulterer?

Shakuntala (to herself). Oh, oh, oh! He even casts doubt on our marriage. The vine of my hope climbed high, but it is broken now.

Sharngarava. Not so.

You scorn the sage who rendered whole
His child befouled, and choked his grief,
Who freely gave you what you stole
And added honour to a thief!

Sharadvata. Enough, Sharngarava. Shakuntala, we have

said what we were sent to say. You hear his words. Answer him.

Shakuntala (*to herself*). He loved me so. He is so changed. Why remind him? Ah, but I must clear my own character. Well, I will try. (*Aloud.*) My dear husband— (*She stops.*) No, he doubts my right to call him that. Your Majesty, it was pure love that opened my poor heart to you in the hermitage. Then you were kind to me and gave me your promise. Is it right for you to speak so now, and to reject me?

King (*stopping his ears*). Peace, peace!

A stream that eats away the bank,
Grows foul, and undermines the tree.
So you would stain your honour, while
You plunge me into misery.

Shakuntala. Very well. If you have acted so because you really fear to touch another man's wife, I will remove your doubts with a token you gave me.

King. An excellent idea!

Shakuntala (*touching her finger*). Oh, oh! The ring is lost. (*She looks sadly at* GAUTAMI.)

Gautami. My child, you worshipped the holy Ganges at the spot where Indra descended. The ring must have fallen there.

King. Ready wit, ready wit!

Shakuntala. Fate is too strong for me there. I will tell you something else.

King. Let me hear what you have to say.

Shakuntala. One day, in the bower of reeds, you were holding a lotus-leaf cup full of water.

King. I hear you.

Shakuntala. At that moment the fawn came up, my adopted son. Then you took pity on him and coaxed him. "Let him drink first," you said. But he did not know you, and he would not come to drink water from your hand. But he liked it afterwards, when I held the very same water. Then you smiled and said: "It is true. Every one trusts his own sort. You both belong to the forest."

King. It is just such women, selfish, sweet, false, that entice fools.

Gautami. You have no right to say that. She grew up in the pious grove. She does not know how to deceive.

King. Old hermit woman,

The female's untaught cunning may be seen
  In beasts, far more in women selfish-wise;
The cuckoo's eggs are left to hatch and rear
  By foster-parents, and away she flies.

Shakuntala (*angrily*). Wretch! You judge all this by your own false heart. Would any other man do what you have done? To hide behind virtue, like a yawning well covered over with grass!

King (*to himself*). But her anger is free from coquetry, because she has lived in the forest. See!

Her glance is straight; her eyes are flashing red;
Her speech is harsh, not drawlingly well-bred;
Her whole lip quivers, seems to shake with cold;
Her frown has straightened eyebrows arching bold.

No, she saw that I was doubtful, and her anger was feigned. Thus

When I refused but now
  Hard-heartedly, to know
Of love or secret vow,
  Her eyes grew red; and so,
Bending her arching brow,
  She fiercely snapped Love's bow.

(*Aloud*.) My good girl, Dushyanta's conduct is known to the whole kingdom, but not this action.

Shakuntala. Well, well. I had my way. I trusted a king, and put myself in his hands. He had a honey face and a heart of stone. (*She covers her face with her dress and weeps*.)

Sharngarava. Thus does unbridled levity burn.

Be slow to love, but yet more slow
  With secret mate;
With those whose hearts we do not know,
  Love turns to hate.

King. Why do you trust this girl, and accuse me of an imaginary crime?

Sharngarava (*disdainfully*). You have learned your wisdom upside down.

It would be monstrous to believe
A girl who never lies;
Trust those who study to deceive
And think it very wise.

King. Aha, my candid friend! Suppose I were to admit that I am such a man. What would happen if I deceived the girl?

Sharngarava. Ruin.

King. It is unthinkable that ruin should fall on Puru's line.

Sharngarava. Why bandy words? We have fulfilled our Father's bidding. We are ready to return.

Leave her or take her, as you will;
She is your wife;
Husbands have power for good or ill
O'er woman's life.

Gautami, lead the way. (*They start to go.*)

Shakuntala. He has deceived me shamelessly. And will you leave me too? (*She starts to follow.*)

Gautami (*turns around and sees her*). Sharngarava, my son, Shakuntala is following us, lamenting piteously. What can the poor child do with a husband base enough to reject her?

Sharngarava (*turns angrily*). You self-willed girl! Do you dare show independence? (SHAKUNTALA *shrinks in fear.*) Listen.

If you deserve such scorn and blame,
What will your father with your shame?
But if you know your vows are pure,
Obey your husband and endure.

Remain. We must go.

King. Hermit, why deceive this woman? Remember:

Night-blossoms open to the moon,
Day-blossoms to the sun;
A man of honour ever strives
Another's wife to shun.

Sharngarava. O King, suppose you had forgotten your former actions in the midst of distractions. Should you now desert your wife—you who fear to fail in virtue?

King. I ask *you* which is the heavier sin:

Not knowing whether I be mad
  Or falsehood be in her,
Shall I desert a faithful wife
  Or turn adulterer?

Chaplain (*considering*). Now if this were done——

King. Instruct me, my teacher.

Chaplain. Let the woman remain in my house until her child is born.

King. Why this?

Chaplain. The chief astrologers have told you that your first child was destined to be an emperor. If the son of the hermit's daughter is born with the imperial birthmarks, then welcome her and introduce her into the palace. Otherwise, she must return to her father.

King. It is good advice, my teacher.

Chaplain (*rising*). Follow me, my daughter.

Shakuntala. O mother earth, give me a grave! (*Exit weeping, with the chaplain, the hermits, and* GAUTAMI. *The king, his memory clouded by the curse, ponders on* SHAKUNTALA.)

Voices behind the scenes. A miracle! A miracle!

King (*listening*). What does this mean? (*Enter the chaplain.*)

Chaplain (*in amazement*). Your Majesty, a wonderful thing has happened.

King. What?

Chaplain. When Kanva's pupils had departed,

She tossed her arms, bemoaned her plight,
  Accused her crushing fate——

King. What then?

Chaplain.

Before our eyes a heavenly light
In woman's form, but shining bright,
  Seized her and vanished straight.

(*All betray astonishment.*)

King. My teacher, we have already settled the matter. Why speculate in vain? Let us seek repose.

Chaplain. Victory to your Majesty. (*Exit*.)

King. Vetravati, I am bewildered. Conduct me to my apartment.

Portress. Follow me, your Majesty.

King (*walks about. To himself*).

With a hermit-wife I had no part,
All memories evade me;
And yet my sad and stricken heart
Would more than half persuade me.

(*Exeunt omnes*.)

ACT VI

SEPARATION FROM SHAKUNTALA

SCENE I.—*In the street before the Palace*

(*Enter the chief of police, two policemen, and a man with his hands bound behind his back.*)

The two policemen (*striking the man*). Now, pickpocket, tell us where you found this ring. It is the king's ring, with letters engraved on it, and it has a magnificent great gem.

Fisherman (*showing fright*). Be merciful, kind gentlemen. I am not guilty of such a crime.

First policeman. No, I suppose the king thought you were a pious Brahman, and made you a present of it.

Fisherman. Listen, please. I am a fisherman, and I live on the Ganges, at the spot where Indra came down.

Second policeman. You thief, we didn't ask for your address or your social position.

Chief. Let him tell a straight story, Suchaka. Don't interrupt.

The two policemen. Yes, chief. Talk, man, talk.

Fisherman. I support my family with things you catch fish with—nets, you know, and hooks, and things.

Chief (*laughing*). You have a sweet trade.

Fisherman. Don't say that, master.

> You can't give up a lowdown trade
> That your ancestors began;
> A butcher butchers things, and yet
> He's the tenderest-hearted man.

Chief. Go on. Go on.

Fisherman. Well, one day I was cutting up a carp. In its maw I see this ring with the magnificent great gem. And then I was just trying to sell it here when you kind gentlemen grabbed me. That is the only way I got it. Now kill me, or find fault with me.

Chief (*smelling the ring*). There is no doubt about it,

Januka. It has been in a fish's maw. It has the real perfume of raw meat. Now we have to find out how he got it. We must go to the palace.

The two policemen (*to the fisherman*). Move on, you cutpurse, move on. (*They walk about.*)

Chief. Suchaka, wait here at the big gate until I come out of the palace. And don't get careless.

The two policemen. Go in, chief. I hope the king will be nice to you.

Chief. Good-bye. (*Exit.*)

Suchaka. Januka, the chief is taking his time.

Januka. You can't just drop in on a king.

Suchaka. Januka, my fingers are itching (*indicating the fisherman*) to kill this cutpurse.

Fisherman. Don't kill a man without any reason, master.

Januka (*looking ahead*). There is the chief, with a written order from the king. (*To the fisherman.*) Now you will see your family, or else you will feed the crows and jackals. (*Enter the chief.*)

Chief. Quick! Quick! (*He breaks off.*)

Fisherman. Oh, oh! I'm a dead man. (*He shows dejection.*)

Chief. Release him, you. Release the fishnet fellow. It is all right, his getting the ring. Our king told me so himself.

Suchaka. All right, chief. He is a dead man come back to life. (*He releases the fisherman.*)

Fisherman (*bowing low to the chief*). Master, I owe you my life. (*He falls at his feet.*)

Chief. Get up, get up! Here is a reward that the king was kind enough to give you. It is worth as much as the ring. Take it. (*He hands the fisherman a bracelet.*)

Fisherman (*joyfully taking it*). Much obliged.

Januka. He *is* much obliged to the king. Just as if he had been taken from the stake and put on an elephant's back.

Suchaka. Chief, the reward shows that the king thought a lot of the ring. The gem must be worth something.

Chief. No, it wasn't the fine gem that pleased the king. It was this way.

The two policemen. Well?

Chief. I think, when the king saw it, he remembered

somebody he loves. You know how dignified he is usually. But as soon as he saw it, he broke down for a moment.

Suchaka. You have done the king a good turn, chief.

Januka. All for the sake of this fish-killer, it seems to me. (*He looks enviously at the fisherman.*)

Fisherman. Take half of it, masters, to pay for something to drink.

Januka. Fisherman, you are the biggest and best friend I've got. The first thing we want, is all the brandy we can hold. Let's go where they keep it. (*Exeunt omnes.*)

SCENE II.—*In the Palace Gardens*

(*Enter* MISHRAKESHI, *flying through the air.*)

Mishrakeshi. I have taken my turn in waiting upon the nymphs. And now I will see what this good king is doing. Shakuntala is like a second self to me, because she is the daughter of Menaka. And it was she who asked me to do this. (*She looks about.*) It is the day of the spring festival. But I see no preparations for a celebration at court. I might learn the reason by my power of divination. But I must do as my friend asked me. Good! I will make myself invisible and stand near these girls who take care of the garden. I shall find out that way. (*She descends to earth. Enter a maid, gazing at a mango branch, and behind her, a second.*)

First maid.

First mango-twig, so pink, so green,
  First living breath of spring,
You are sacrificed as soon as seen,
  A festival offering.

Second maid. What are you chirping about to yourself, little cuckoo?

First maid. Why, little bee, you know that the cuckoo goes crazy with delight when she sees the mango-blossom.

Second maid (*joyfully*). Oh, has the spring really come?

First maid. Yes, little bee. And this is the time when you too buzz about in crazy joy.

Second maid. Hold me, dear, while I stand on tiptoe and offer this blossom to Love, the divine.

First maid. If I do, you must give me half the reward of the offering.

Second maid. That goes without saying, dear. We two are one. (*She leans on her friend and takes the mango-blossom.*) Oh, see! The mango-blossom hasn't opened, but it has broken the sheath, so it is fragrant. (*She brings her hands together.*) I worship mighty Love.

O mango-twig I give to Love
  As arrow for his bow,
Most sovereign of his arrows five,
  Strike maiden-targets low.

(*She throws the twig. Enter the chamberlain.*)

Chamberlain (*angrily*). Stop, silly girl. The king has strictly forbidden the spring festival. Do you dare pluck the mango-blossoms?

The two maids (*frightened*). Forgive us, sir. We did not know.

Chamberlain. What! You have not heard the king's command, which is obeyed even by the trees of spring and the creatures that dwell in them. See!

The mango branches are in bloom,
  Yet pollen does not form;
The cuckoo's song sticks in his throat,
  Although the days are warm;

The amaranth-bud is formed, and yet
  Its power of growth is gone;
The love-god timidly puts by
  The arrow he has drawn.

Mishrakeshi. There is no doubt of it. This good king has wonderful power.

First maid. A few days ago, sir, we were sent to his Majesty by his brother-in-law Mitravasu to decorate the garden. That is why we have heard nothing of this affair.

Chamberlain. You must not do so again.

The two maids. But we are curious. If we girls may know about it, pray tell us, sir. Why did his Majesty forbid the spring festival?

Mishrakeshi. Kings are fond of celebrations. There must be some good reason.

Chamberlain (*to himself*). It is in everybody's mouth. Why should I not tell it? (*Aloud*.) Have you heard the gossip concerning Shakuntala's rejection?

The two maids. Yes, sir. The king's brother-in-law told us, up to the point where the ring was recovered.

Chamberlain. There is little more to tell. When his Majesty saw the ring, he remembered that he had indeed contracted a secret marriage with Shakuntala, and had rejected her under a delusion. And then he fell a prey to remorse.

He hates the things he loved; he intermits
The daily audience, nor in judgment sits;
Spends sleepless nights in tossing on his bed;
At times, when he by courtesy is led
To address a lady, speaks another name,
Then stands for minutes, sunk in helpless shame.

Mishrakeshi. I am glad to hear it.

Chamberlain. His Majesty's sorrow has forbidden the festival.

The two maids. It is only right.

A voice behind the scenes. Follow me.

Chamberlain (*listening*). Ah, his Majesty approaches. Go, and attend to your duties. (*Exeunt the two maids. Enter the king, wearing a dress indicative of remorse; the clown, and the portress*.)

Chamberlain (*observing the king*). A beautiful figure charms in whatever state. Thus, his Majesty is pleasing even in his sorrow. For

All ornament is laid aside; he wears
  One golden bracelet on his wasted arm;
His lip is scorched by sighs; and sleepless cares
  Redden his eyes. Yet all can work no harm
On that magnificent beauty, wasting, but
Gaining in brilliance, like a diamond cut.

Mishrakeshi (*observing the king*). No wonder Shakuntala pines for him, even though he dishonoured her by his rejection of her.

King (*walks about slowly, sunk in thought*).

Alas! My smitten heart, that once lay sleeping,
Heard in its dreams my fawn-eyed love's laments,
And wakened now, awakens but to weeping,
To bitter grief, and tears of penitence.

Mishrakeshi. That is the poor girl's fate.

Clown (*to himself*). He has got his Shakuntala-sickness again. I wish I knew how to cure him.

Chamberlain (*advancing*). Victory to your Majesty. I have examined the garden. Your Majesty may visit its retreats.

King. Vetravati, tell the minister Pishuna in my name that a sleepless night prevents me from mounting the throne of judgment. He is to investigate the citizens' business and send me a memorandum.

Portress. Yes, your Majesty. (*Exit.*)

King. And you, Parvatayana, return to your post of duty.

Chamberlain. Yes, your Majesty. (*Exit.*)

Clown. You have got rid of the vermin. Now amuse yourself in this garden. It is delightful with the passing of the cold weather.

King (*sighing*). My friend, the proverb makes no mistake. Misfortune finds the weak spot. See!

No sooner did the darkness lift
That clouded memory's power,
Than the god of love prepared his bow
And shot the mango-flower.

No sooner did the ring recall
My banished maiden dear,
No sooner do I vainly weep
For her, than spring is here.

Clown. Wait a minute, man. I will destroy Love's arrow with my stick. (*He raises his stick and strikes at the mango branch.*)

King (*smiling*). Enough! I see your pious power. My friend, where shall I sit now to comfort my eyes with the vines? They remind me somehow of her.

Clown. Well, you told one of the maids, the clever painter, that you would spend this hour in the bower of spring-creepers. And you asked her to bring you there the picture of the lady Shakuntala which you painted on a tablet.

King. It is my only consolation. Lead the way to the bower of spring-creepers.

Clown. Follow me. (*They walk about.* MISHRAKESHI *follows.*) Here is the bower of spring-creepers, with its jewelled benches. Its loneliness seems to bid you a silent welcome. Let us go in and sit down. (*They do so.*)

Mishrakeshi. I will hide among the vines and see the dear girl's picture. Then I shall be able to tell her how deep her husband's love is. (*She hides.*)

King (*sighing*). I remember it all now, my friend. I told you how I first met Shakuntala. It is true, you were not with me when I rejected her. But I had told you of her at the first. Had you forgotten, as I did?

Mishrakeshi. This shows that a king should not be separated a single moment from some intimate friend.

Clown. No, I didn't forget. But when you had told the whole story, you said it was a joke and there was nothing in it. And I was fool enough to believe you. No, this is the work of fate.

Mishrakeshi. It must be.

King (*after meditating a moment*). Help me, my friend.

Clown. But, man, this isn't right at all. A good man never lets grief get the upper hand. The mountains are calm even in a tempest.

King. My friend, I am quite forlorn. I keep thinking of her pitiful state when I rejected her. Thus:

> When I denied her, then she tried
> To join her people. "Stay," one cried,
> Her father's representative.
> She stopped, she turned, she could but give
> A tear-dimmed glance to heartless me—
> That arrow burns me poisonously.

Mishrakeshi. How his fault distresses him!

Clown. Well, I don't doubt it was some heavenly being that carried her away.

King. Who else would dare to touch a faithful wife? Her friends told me that Menaka was her mother. My heart persuades me that it was she, or companions of hers, who carried Shakuntala away.

Mishrakeshi. His madness was wonderful, not his awakening reason.

Clown. But in that case, you ought to take heart. You will meet her again.

King. How so?

Clown. Why, a mother or a father cannot long bear to see a daughter separated from her husband.

King. My friend,

And was it phantom, madness, dream,
Or fatal retribution stern?
My hopes fell down a precipice
And never, never will return.

Clown. Don't talk that way. Why, the ring shows that incredible meetings do happen.

King (*looking at the ring*). This ring deserves pity. It has fallen from a heaven hard to earn.

Your virtue, ring, like mine,
Is proved to be but small;
Her pink-nailed finger sweet
You clasped. How could you fall?

Mishrakeshi. If it were worn on any other hand, it would deserve pity. My dear girl, you are far away. I am the only one to hear these delightful words.

Clown. Tell me how you put the ring on her finger.

Mishrakeshi. He speaks as if prompted by my curiosity.

King. Listen, my friend. When I left the pious grove for the city, my darling wept and said: "But how long will you remember us, dear?"

Clown. And then you said——

King. Then I put this engraved ring on her finger, and said to her——

Clown. Well, what?

King. Count every day one letter of my name;
Before you reach the end, dear,
Will come to lead you to my palace halls
A guide whom I shall send, dear.

Then, through my madness, it fell out cruelly.

Mishrakeshi. It was too charming an agreement to be frustrated by fate.

Clown. But how did it get into a carp's mouth, as if it had been a fish-hook?

King. While she was worshipping the Ganges at Shachi-tirtha, it fell.

Clown. I see.

Mishrakeshi. That is why the virtuous king doubted his marriage with poor Shakuntala. Yet such love does not ask for a token. How could it have been?

King. Well, I can only reproach this ring.

Clown (*smiling*). And I will reproach this stick of mine. Why are you crooked when I am straight?

King (*not hearing him*).

How could you fail to linger
On her soft, tapering finger,
  And in the water fall?

And yet

Things lifeless know not beauty;
But I—I scorned my duty,
  The sweetest task of all.

Mishrakeshi. He has given the answer which I had ready.

Clown. But that is no reason why I should starve to death.

King (*not heeding*). O my darling, my heart burns with repentance because I abandoned you without reason. Take pity on me. Let me see you again. (*Enter a maid with a tablet.*)

Maid. Your Majesty, here is the picture of our lady. (*She produces the tablet.*)

King (*gazing at it*). It is a beautiful picture. See!

A graceful arch of brows above great eyes;
Lips bathed in darting, smiling light that flies
Reflected from white teeth; a mouth as red
As red karkandhu-fruit; love's brightness shed
O'er all her face in bursts of liquid charm—
The picture speaks, with living beauty warm.

Clown (*looking at it*). The sketch is full of sweet meaning. My eyes seem to stumble over its uneven surface. What more can I say? I expect to see it come to life, and I feel like speaking to it.

Mishrakeshi. The king is a clever painter. I seem to see the dear girl before me.

King. My friend,

What in the picture is not fair,
Is badly done;
Yet something of her beauty there,
I feel, is won.

Mishrakeshi. This is natural, when love is increased by remorse.

King (*sighing*).

I treated her with scorn and loathing ever;
Now o'er her pictured charms my heart will burst:
A traveller I, who scorned the mighty river,
And seeks in the mirage to quench his thirst.

Clown. There are three figures in the picture, and they are all beautiful. Which one is the lady Shakuntala?

Mishrakeshi. The poor fellow never saw her beauty. His eyes are useless, for she never came before them.

King. Which one do you think?

Clown (*observing closely*). I think it is this one, leaning against the creeper which she has just sprinkled. Her face is hot and the flowers are dropping from her hair; for the ribbon is loosened. Her arms droop like weary branches; she has loosened her girdle, and she seems a little fatigued. This, I think, is the lady Shakuntala, the others are her friends.

King. You are good at guessing. Besides, here are proofs of my love.

See where discolorations faint
Of loving handling tell;
And here the swelling of the paint
Shows where my sad tears fell.

Chaturika, I have not finished the background. Go, get the brushes.

Maid. Please hold the picture, Madhavya, while I am gone.

King. I will hold it. (*He does so. Exit maid.*)

Clown. What are you going to add?

Mishrakeshi. Surely, every spot that the dear girl loved.

King. Listen, my friend.

The stream of Maliní, and on its sands
The swan-pairs resting; holy foot-hill lands
Of great Himalaya's sacred ranges, where
The yaks are seen; and under trees that bear
Bark hermit-dresses on their branches high,
A doe that on the buck's horn rubs her eye.

Clown (*aside*). To hear him talk, I should think he was going to fill up the picture with heavy-bearded hermits.

King. And another ornament that Shakuntala loved I have forgotten to paint.

Clown. What?

Mishrakeshi. Something natural for a girl living in the forest.

King.

The siris-blossom, fastened o'er her ear,
Whose stamens brush her cheek;
The lotus-chain like autumn moonlight soft
Upon her bosom meek.

Clown. But why does she cover her face with fingers lovely as the pink water-lily? She seems frightened. (*He looks more closely.*) I see. Here is a bold, bad bee. He steals honey, and so he flies to her lotus-face.

King. Drive him away.

Clown. It is your affair to punish evil-doers.

King. True. O welcome guest of the flowering vine, why do you waste your time in buzzing here?

Your faithful, loving queen,
Perched on a flower, athirst,
Is waiting for you still,
Nor tastes the honey first.

Mishrakeshi. A gentlemanly way to drive him off!

Clown. This kind are obstinate, even when you warn them.

King (*angrily*). Will you not obey my command? Then listen:

'Tis sweet as virgin blossoms on a tree,
The lip I kissed in love-feasts tenderly;
Sting that dear lip, O bee, with cruel power,
And you shall be imprisoned in a flower.

Clown. Well, he doesn't seem afraid of your dreadful punishment. (*Laughing. To himself.*) The man is crazy, and I am just as bad, from associating with him.

King. Will he not go, though I warn him?

Mishrakeshi. Love works a curious change even in a brave man.

Clown (*aloud*). It is only a picture, man.

King. A picture?

Mishrakeshi. I too understand it now. But to him, thoughts are real experiences.

King. You have done an ill-natured thing.

When I was happy in the sight,
  And when my heart was warm,
You brought sad memories back, and made
  My love a painted form. (*He sheds a tear.*)

Mishrakeshi. Fate plays strangely with him.

King. My friend, how can I endure a grief that has no respite?

I cannot sleep at night
  And meet her dreaming;
I cannot see the sketch
  While tears are streaming.

Mishrakeshi. My friend, you have indeed atoned—and in her friend's presence—for the pain you caused by rejecting dear Shakuntala. (*Enter the maid* CHATURIKA.)

Maid. Your Majesty, I was coming back with the box of paint-brushes——

King. Well?

Maid. I met Queen Vasumati with the maid Pingalika. And the queen snatched the box from me, saying: "I will take it to the king myself."

Clown. How did you escape?

Maid. The queen's dress caught on a vine. And while her maid was setting her free, I excused myself in a hurry.

A voice behind the scenes. Follow me, your Majesty.

Clown (*listening*). Man, the she-tiger of the palace is making a spring on her prey. She means to make one mouthful of the maid.

King. My friend, the queen has come because she feels touched in her honour. You had better take care of this picture.

Clown. " And yourself," you might add. (*He takes the picture and rises.*) If you get out of the trap alive, call for me at the Cloud Balcony. And I will hide the thing there so that nothing but a pigeon could find it. (*Exit on the run.*)

Mishrakeshi. Though his heart is given to another, he is courteous to his early flame. He is a constant friend. (*Enter the portress with a document.*)

Portress. Victory to your Majesty.

King. Vetravati, did you not meet Queen Vasumati?

Portress. Yes, your Majesty. But she turned back when she saw that I carried a document.

King. The queen knows times and seasons. She will not interrupt business.

Portress. Your Majesty, the minister sends word that in the press of various business he has attended to only one citizen's suit. This he has reduced to writing for your Majesty's perusal.

King. Give me the document. (*The portress does so.*)

King (*reads*). " Be it known to his Majesty. A seafaring merchant named Dhanavriddhi has been lost in a shipwreck. He is childless, and his property, amounting to several millions, reverts to the crown. Will his Majesty take action? " (*Sadly.*) It is dreadful to be childless. Vetravati, he had great riches. There must be several wives. Let inquiry be made. There may be a wife who is with child.

Portress. We have this moment heard that a merchant's daughter of Saketa is his wife. And she is soon to become a mother.

King. The child shall receive the inheritance. Go, inform the minister.

Portress. Yes, your Majesty. (*She starts to go.*)

King. Wait a moment.

Portress (*turning back*). Yes, your Majesty.

King. After all, what does it matter whether he have issue or not?

Let King Dushyanta be proclaimed
To every sad soul kin
That mourns a kinsman loved and lost,
Yet did not plunge in sin.

Portress. The proclamation shall be made. (*She goes out and soon returns*.) Your Majesty, the royal proclamation was welcomed by the populace as is a timely shower.

King (*sighing deeply*). Thus, when issue fails, wealth passes, on the death of the head of the family, to a stranger. When I die, it will be so with the glory of Puru's line.

Portress. Heaven avert the omen!

King. Alas! I despised the happiness that offered itself to me.

Mishrakeshi. Without doubt, he has dear Shakuntala in mind when he thus reproaches himself.

King. Could I forsake the virtuous wife
Who held my best, my future life
And cherished it for glorious birth,
As does the seed-receiving earth?

Mishrakeshi. She will not long be forsaken.

Maid (*to the portress*). Mistress, the minister's report has doubled our lord's remorse. Go to the Cloud Balcony and bring Madhavya to dispel his grief.

Portress. A good suggestion. (*Exit*.)

King. Alas! The ancestors of Dushyanta are in a doubtful case.

For I am childless, and they do not know,
When I am gone, what child of theirs will bring
The scriptural oblation; and their tears
Already mingle with my offering.

Mishrakeshi. He is screened from the light, and is in darkness.

Maid. Do not give way to grief, your Majesty. You are in the prime of your years, and the birth of a son to one of your other wives will make you blameless before your ancestors. (*To herself*.) He does not heed me. The proper medicine is needed for any disease.

King (*betraying his sorrow*). Surely,

The royal line that flowed
A river pure and grand,
Dies in the childless king,
Like streams in desert sand. (*He swoons.*)

Maid (*in distress*). Oh, sir, come to yourself.

Mishrakeshi. Shall I make him happy now? No, I heard the mother of the gods consoling Shakuntala. She said that the gods, impatient for the sacrifice, would soon cause him to welcome his true wife. I must delay no longer. I will comfort dear Shakuntala with my tidings. (*Exit through the air.*)

A voice behind the scenes. Help, help!

King (*comes to himself and listens*). It sounds as if Madhavya were in distress.

Maid. Your Majesty, I hope that Pingalika and the other maids did not catch poor Madhavya with the picture in his hands.

King. Go, Chaturika. Reprove the queen in my name for not controlling her servants.

Maid. Yes, your Majesty. (*Exit.*)

The voice. Help, help!

King. The Brahman's voice seems really changed by fear. Who waits without? (*Enter the chamberlain.*)

Chamberlain. Your Majesty commands?

King. See why poor Madhavya is screaming so.

Chamberlain. I will see. (*He goes out, and returns trembling.*)

King. Parvatayana, I hope it is nothing very dreadful.

Chamberlain. I hope not.

King. Then why do you tremble so? For

Why should the trembling, born
Of age, increasing, seize
Your limbs and bid them shake
Like fig-leaves in the breeze?

Chamberlain. Save your friend, O King!

King. From what?

Chamberlain. From great danger.

King. Speak plainly, man.

Chamberlain. On the Cloud Balcony, open to the four winds of heaven——

King. What has happened there?

Chamberlain.

> While he was resting on its height,
> Which palace peacocks in their flight
> Can hardly reach, he seemed to be
> Snatched up—by what, we could not see.

King (*rising quickly*). My very palace is invaded by evil creatures. To be a king, is to be a disappointed man.

> The moral stumblings of mine own,
> The daily slips, are scarcely known;
> Who then that rules a kingdom, can
> Guide every deed of every man?

The voice. Hurry, hurry!

King (*hears the voice and quickens his steps*). Have no fear, my friend.

The voice. Have no fear! When something has got me by the back of the neck, and is trying to break my bones like a piece of sugar-cane!

King (*looks about*). A bow! a bow! (*Enter a Greek woman with a bow.*)

Greek woman. A bow and arrows, your Majesty. And here are the finger-guards. (*The king takes the bow and arrows.*)

Another voice behind the scenes.

> Writhe, while I drink the red blood flowing clear
> And kill you, as a tiger kills a deer;
> Let King Dushyanta grasp his bow; but how
> Can all his kingly valour save you now?

King (*angrily*). He scorns me, too! In one moment, miserable demon, you shall die. (*Stringing his bow.*) Where is the stairway, Parvatayana?

Chamberlain. Here, your Majesty. (*All make haste.*)

King (*looking about*). There is no one here.

The Clown's voice. Save me, save me! I see you, if you can't see me. I am a mouse in the claws of the cat. I am done for.

King. You are proud of your invisibility. But shall not my arrow see you? Stand still. Do not hope to escape by clinging to my friend.

My arrow, flying when the bow is bent,
Shall slay the wretch and spare the innocent;
When milk is mixed with water in a cup,
Swans leave the water, and the milk drink up.

(*He takes aim. Enter* MATALI *and the clown.*)

Matali. O King, as Indra, king of the gods, commands,

Seek foes among the evil powers alone;
For them your bow should bend;
Not cruel shafts, but glances soft and kind
Should fall upon a friend.

King (*hastily withdrawing the arrow*). It is Matali. Welcome to the charioteer of heaven's king.

Clown. Well! He came within an inch of butchering me. And you welcome him.

Matali (*smiling*). Hear, O King, for what purpose Indra sends me to you.

King. I am all attention.

Matali. There is a host of demons who call themselves Invincible—the brood of Kalanemi.

King. So Narada has told me.

Matali.

Heaven's king is powerless; you shall smite
His foes in battle soon;
Darkness that overcomes the day,
Is scattered by the moon.

Take your bow at once, enter my heavenly chariot, and set forth for victory.

King. I am grateful for the honour which Indra shows me. But why did you act thus toward Madhavya?

Matali. I will tell you. I saw that you were overpowered by some inner sorrow, and acted thus to rouse you. For

The spurnèd snake will swell his hood;
Fire blazes when 'tis stirred;
Brave men are roused to fighting mood
By some insulting word.

King. Friend Madhavya, I must obey the bidding of heaven's king. Go, acquaint the minister Pishuna with the matter, and add these words of mine:

Your wisdom only shall control
The kingdom for a time;
My bow is strung; a distant goal
Calls me, and tasks sublime.

Clown. Very well. (*Exit.*)

Matali. Enter the chariot. (*The king does so. Exeunt omnes.*)

ACT VII

(*Enter, in a chariot that flies through the air, the king and* MATALI.)

King. Matali, though I have done what Indra commanded, I think myself an unprofitable servant, when I remember his most gracious welcome.

Matali. O King, know that each considers himself the other's debtor. For

You count the service given
Small by the welcome paid,
Which to the king of heaven
Seems mean for such brave aid.

King. Ah, no! For the honour given me at parting went far beyond imagination. Before the gods, he seated me beside him on his throne. And then

He smiled, because his son Jayanta's heart
Beat quicker, by the self-same wish oppressed,
And placed about my neck the heavenly wreath
Still fragrant from the sandal on his breast.

Matali. But what do you not deserve from heaven's king? Remember:

Twice, from peace-loving Indra's sway
The demon-thorn was plucked away:
First, by Man-lion's crooked claws;
Again, by your smooth shafts to-day.

King. This merely proves Indra's majesty. Remember:

All servants owe success in enterprise
To honour paid before the great deed's done;
Could dawn defeat the darkness otherwise
Than resting on the chariot of the sun?

Matali. The feeling becomes you. (*After a little*.) See, O King! Your glory has the happiness of being published abroad in heaven.

With colours used by nymphs of heaven
  To make their beauty shine,
Gods write upon the surface given
  Of many a magic vine,
As worth their song, the simple story
Of those brave deeds that made your glory.

King. Matali, when I passed before, I was intent on fighting the demons, and did not observe this region. Tell me. In which path of the winds are we?

Matali.

It is the windpath sanctified
By holy Vishnu's second stride;
Which, freed from dust of passion, ever
Upholds the threefold heavenly river;
And, driving them with reins of light,
Guides the stars in wheeling flight.

King. That is why serenity pervades me, body and soul. (*He observes the path taken by the chariot.*) It seems that we have descended into the region of the clouds.

Matali. How do you perceive it?

King.

Plovers that fly from mountain-caves,
Steeds that quick-flashing lightning laves,
And chariot-wheels that drip with spray—
A path o'er pregnant clouds betray.

Matali. You are right. And in a moment you will be in the world over which you bear rule.

King (*looking down*). Matali, our quick descent gives the world of men a mysterious look. For

The plains appear to melt and fall
From mountain peaks that grow more tall;
The trunks of trees no longer hide
Nor in their leafy nests abide;
The river network now is clear,
For smaller streams at last appear:
It seems as if some being threw
The world to me, for clearer view.

Matali. You are a good observer, O King. (*He looks down, awe-struck.*) There is a noble loveliness in the earth.

King. Matali, what mountain is this, its flanks sinking into the eastern and into the western sea? It drips liquid gold like a cloud at sunset.

Matali. O King, this is Gold Peak, the mountain of the fairy centaurs. Here it is that ascetics most fully attain to magic powers. See!

The ancient sage, Marichi's son,
Child of the Uncreated One,
Father of superhuman life,
Dwells here austerely with his wife.

King (*reverently*). I must not neglect the happy chance. I cannot go farther until I have walked humbly about the holy one.

Matali. It is a worthy thought, O King. (*The chariot descends*.) We have come down to earth.

King (*astonished*). Matali,

The wheels are mute on whirling rim;
Unstirred, the dust is lying there;
We do not bump the earth, but skim:
Still, still we seem to fly through air.

Matali. Such is the glory of the chariot which obeys you and Indra.

King. In which direction lies the hermitage of Marichi's son?

Matali (*pointing*). See!

Where stands the hermit, horridly austere,
Whom clinging vines are choking, tough and sere;
Half-buried in an ant-hill that has grown
About him, standing post-like and alone;
Sun-staring with dim eyes that know no rest,
The dead skin of a serpent on his breast:
So long he stood unmoved, insensate there
That birds build nests within his mat of hair.

King (*gazing*). All honour to one who mortifies the flesh so terribly.

Matali (*checking the chariot*). We have entered the hermitage of the ancient sage, whose wife Aditi tends the coral-trees.

King. Here is deeper contentment than in heaven. I seem plunged in a pool of nectar.

Matali (*stopping the chariot*). Descend, O King.

King (*descending*). But how will you fare?

Matali. The chariot obeys the word of command. I too will descend. (*He does so.*) Before you, O King, are the groves where the holiest hermits lead their self-denying life.

King. I look with amazement both at their simplicity and at what they might enjoy.

Their appetites are fed with air
Where grows whatever is most fair;
They bathe religiously in pools
Which golden lily-pollen cools;
They pray within a jewelled home,
Are chaste where nymphs of heaven roam:
They mortify desire and sin
With things that others fast to win.

Matali. The desires of the great aspire high. (*He walks about and speaks to some one not visible.*) Ancient Shakalya, how is Marichi's holy son occupied? (*He listens.*) What do you say? That he is explaining to Aditi, in answer to her question, the duties of a faithful wife? My matter must await a fitter time. (*He turns to the king.*) Wait here, O King, in the shade of the ashoka tree, till I have announced your coming to the sire of Indra.

King. Very well. (*Exit* MATALI. *The king's arm throbs, a happy omen.*)

I dare not hope for what I pray;
  Why thrill—in vain?
For heavenly bliss once thrown away
  Turns into pain.

A voice behind the scenes. Don't! You mustn't be so foolhardy. Oh, you are always the same.

King (*listening*). No naughtiness could feel at home in this spot. Who draws such a rebuke upon himself? (*He looks towards the sound. In surprise.*) It is a child, but no child in strength. And two hermit-women are trying to control him.

He drags a struggling lion cub,
The lioness' milk half-sucked, half-missed,
Towzles his mane, and tries to drub
Him tame with small, imperious fist.

(*Enter a small boy, as described, and two hermit-women.*)

Boy. Open your mouth, cub. I want to count your teeth.

First woman. Naughty boy, why do you torment our pets? They are like children to us. Your energy seems to take the form of striking something. No wonder the hermits call you All-tamer.

King. Why should my heart go out to this boy as if he were my own son? (*He reflects.*) No doubt my childless state makes me sentimental.

Second woman. The lioness will spring at you if you don't let her baby go.

Boy (*smiling*). Oh, I'm dreadfully scared. (*He bites his lip.*)

King (*in surprise*).

The boy is seed of fire
Which, when it grows, will burn;
A tiny spark that soon
To awful flame may turn.

First woman. Let the little lion go, dear. I will give you another plaything.

Boy. Where is it? Give it to me. (*He stretches out his hand.*)

King (*looking at the hand.*) He has one of the imperial birthmarks! For

Between the eager fingers grow
The close-knit webs together drawn,
Like some lone lily opening slow
To meet the kindling blush of dawn.

Second woman. Suvrata, we can't make him stop by talking. Go. In my cottage you will find a painted clay peacock that belongs to the hermit-boy Mankanaka. Bring him that.

First woman. I will. (*Exit.*)

Boy. Meanwhile I'll play with this one.

Hermit-woman (*looks and laughs*). Let him go.

King. My heart goes out to this wilful child. (*Sighing.*)

They show their little buds of teeth
  In peals of causeless laughter;
They hide their trustful heads beneath
  Your heart. And stumbling after
Come sweet, unmeaning sounds that sing
  To you. The father warms
And loves the very dirt they bring
  Upon their little forms.

Hermit-woman (*shaking her finger*). Won't you mind me? (*She looks about.*) Which one of the hermit-boys is here? (*She sees the king.*) Oh, sir, please come here and free this lion cub. The little rascal is tormenting him, and I can't make him let go.

King. Very well. (*He approaches, smiling.*) O little son of a great sage!

Your conduct in this place apart,
  Is most unfit;
'Twould grieve your father's pious heart
  And trouble it.

To animals he is as good
  As good can be;
You spoil it, like a black snake's brood
  In sandal tree.

Hermit-woman. But, sir, he is not the son of a hermit.

King. So it would seem, both from his looks and his actions. But in this spot, I had no suspicion of anything else. (*He loosens the boy's hold on the cub, and touching him, says to himself.*)

It makes me thrill to touch the boy,
  The stranger's son, to me unknown;
What measureless content must fill
  The man who calls the child his own!

Hermit-woman (*looking at the two*). Wonderful! wonderful!

King. Why do you say that, mother?

Hermit-woman. I am astonished to see how much the boy looks like you, sir. You are not related. Besides, he is a perverse little creature and he does not know you. Yet he takes no dislike to you.

King (*caressing the boy*). Mother, if he is not the son of a hermit, what is his family?

Hermit-woman. The family of Puru.

King (*to himself*). He is of one family with me! Then could my thought be true? (*Aloud.*) But this is the custom of Puru's line:

> In glittering palaces they dwell
> While men, and rule the country well;
> Then make the grove their home in age,
> And die in austere hermitage.

But how could human beings, of their own mere motion, attain this spot?

Hermit-woman. You are quite right, sir. But the boy's mother was related to a nymph, and she bore her son in the pious grove of the father of the gods.

King (*to himself*). Ah, a second ground for hope. (*Aloud.*) What was the name of the good king whose wife she was?

Hermit-woman. Who would speak his name? He rejected his true wife.

King (*to himself*). This story points at me. Suppose I ask the boy for his mother's name. (*He reflects.*) No, it is wrong to concern myself with one who may be another's wife. (*Enter the first woman, with the clay peacock.*)

First woman. Look, All-tamer. Here is the bird, the *shakunta.* Isn't the *shakunta* lovely?

Boy (*looks about*). Where is my mamma? (*The two women burst out laughing.*)

First woman. It sounded like her name, and deceived him. He loves his mother.

Second woman. She said: "See how pretty the peacock is." That is all.

King (*to himself*). His mother's name is Shakuntala! But names are alike. I trust this hope may not prove a disappointment in the end, like a mirage.

Boy. I like this little peacock, sister. Can it fly? (*He seizes the toy.*)

First woman (looks at the boy. Anxiously). Oh, the amulet is not on his wrist.

King. Do not be anxious, mother. It fell while he was struggling with the lion cub. (*He starts to pick it up.*)

The two women. Oh, don't, don't! (*They look at him.*) He has touched it! (*Astonished, they lay their hands on their bosoms, and look at each other.*)

King. Why did you try to prevent me?

First woman. Listen, your Majesty. This is a divine and most potent charm, called the Invincible. Marichi's holy son gave it to the baby when the birth-ceremony was performed. If it falls on the ground, no one may touch it except the boy's parents or the boy himself.

King. And if another touch it?

First woman. It becomes a serpent and stings him.

King. Did you ever see this happen to any one else?

Both women. More than once.

King (joyfully). Then why may I not welcome my hopes fulfilled at last? (*He embraces the boy.*)

Second woman. Come, Suvrata. Shakuntala is busy with her religious duties. We must go and tell her what has happened. (*Exeunt ambo.*)

Boy. Let me go. I want to see my mother.

King. My son, you shall go with me to greet your mother.

Boy. Dushyanta is my father, not you.

King (smiling). You show I am right by contradicting me.

(*Enter* SHAKUNTALA, *wearing her hair in a single braid.*)

Shakuntala (doubtfully). I have heard that All-tamer's amulet did not change when it should have done so. But I do not trust my own happiness. Yet perhaps it is as Mishrakeshi told me. (*She walks about.*)

King (looking at SHAKUNTALA. *With plaintive joy).* It is she. It is Shakuntala.

The pale, worn face, the careless dress,
  The single braid,
Show her still true, me pitiless,
  The long vow paid.

Shakuntala (seeing the king pale with remorse. Doubtfully). It is not my husband. Who is the man that soils my boy with his caresses? The amulet should protect him.

Boy (*running to his mother*). Mother, he is a man that belongs to other people. And he calls me his son.

King. My darling, the cruelty I showed you has turned to happiness. Will you not recognise me?

Shakuntala (*to herself*). Oh, my heart, believe it. Fate struck hard, but its envy is gone and pity takes its place. It is my husband.

King.

Black madness flies;
Comes memory;
Before my eyes
My love I see.

Eclipse flees far;
Light follows soon;
The loving star
Draws to the moon.

Shakuntala. Victory, victo—— (*Tears choke her utterance.*)

King.

The tears would choke you, sweet, in vain;
My soul with victory is fed,
Because I see your face again—
No jewels, but the lips are red.

Boy. Who is he, mother?

Shakuntala. Ask fate, my child. (*She weeps.*)

King.

Dear, graceful wife, forget;
Let the sin vanish;
Strangely did madness strive
Reason to banish.

Thus blindness works in men,
Love's joy to shake;
Spurning a garland, lest
It prove a snake. (*He falls at her feet.*)

Shakuntala. Rise, my dear husband. Surely, it was some old sin of mine that broke my happiness—though it has turned again to happiness. Otherwise, how could you, dear, have acted so? You are so kind. (*The king rises.*) But what brought back the memory of your suffering wife?

King. I will tell you when I have plucked out the dart of sorrow.

'Twas madness, sweet, that could let slip
A tear to burden your dear lip;
On graceful lashes seen to-day,
I wipe it, and our grief, away. (*He does so.*)

Shakuntala (*sees more clearly and discovers the ring*). My husband, it is the ring!

King. Yes. And when a miracle recovered it, my memory returned.

Shakuntala. That was why it was so impossible for me to win your confidence.

King. Then let the vine receive her flower, as earnest of her union with spring.

Shakuntala. I do not trust it. I would rather you wore it. (*Enter* MATALI.)

Matali. I congratulate you, O King, on reunion with your wife and on seeing the face of your son.

King. My desires bear sweeter fruit because fulfilled through a friend. Matali, was not this matter known to Indra?

Matali (*smiling*). What is hidden from the gods? Come. Marichi's holy son, Kashyapa, wishes to see you.

King. My dear wife, bring our son. I could not appear without you before the holy one.

Shakuntala. I am ashamed to go before such parents with my husband.

King. It is the custom in times of festival. Come. (*They walk about.* KASHYAPA *appears seated, with* ADITI.)

Kashyapa (*looking at the king*). Aditi,

'Tis King Dushyanta, he who goes before
  Your son in battle, and who rules the earth,
Whose bow makes Indra's weapon seem no more
  Than a fine plaything, lacking sterner worth.

Aditi. His valour might be inferred from his appearance.

Matali. O King, the parents of the gods look upon you with a glance that betrays parental fondness. Approach them.

King. Matali,

Sprung from the Creator's children, do I see
Great Kashyapa and Mother Aditi?
The pair that did produce the sun in heaven,
To which each year twelve changing forms are given;
That brought the king of all the gods to birth,
Who rules in heaven, in hell, and on the earth;
That Vishnu, than the Uncreated higher,
Chose as his parents with a fond desire.

Matali. It is indeed they.

King (*falling before them*). Dushyanta, servant of Indra, does reverence to you both.

Kashyapa. My son, rule the earth long.

Aditi. And be invincible. (SHAKUNTALA *and her son fall at their feet.*)

Kashyapa. My daughter,

Your husband equals Indra, king
Of gods; your son is like his son;
No further blessing need I bring:
Win bliss such as his wife has won.

Aditi. My child, keep the favour of your husband. And may this fine boy be an honour to the families of both parents. Come, let us be seated. (*All seat themselves.*)

Kashyapa (*indicating one after the other*).

Faithful Shakuntala, the boy,
And you, O King, I see
A trinity to bless the world—
Faith, Treasure, Piety.

King. Holy one, your favour shown to us is without parallel. You granted the fulfilment of our wishes before you called us to your presence. For, holy one,

The flower comes first, and then the fruit;
The clouds appear before the rain;
Effect comes after cause; but you
First helped, then made your favour plain.

Matali. O King, such is the favour shown by the parents of the world.

King. Holy one, I married this your maid-servant by the voluntary ceremony. When after a time her relatives brought her to me, my memory failed and I rejected her. In so doing, I sinned against Kanva, who is kin to you. But afterwards, when I saw the ring, I perceived that I had married her. And this seems very wonderful to me.

> Like one who doubts an elephant,
> Though seeing him stride by,
> And yet believes when he has seen
> The footprints left; so I.

Kashyapa. My son, do not accuse yourself of sin. Your infatuation was inevitable. Listen.

King. I am all attention.

Kashyapa. When the nymph Menaka descended to earth and received Shakuntala, afflicted at her rejection, she came to Aditi. Then I perceived the matter by my divine insight. I saw that the unfortunate girl had been rejected by her rightful husband because of Durvasas' curse. And that the curse would end when the ring came to light.

King (*with a sigh of relief. To himself*). Then I am free from blame.

Shakuntala (*to herself*). Thank heaven! My husband did not reject me of his own accord. He really did not remember me. I suppose I did not hear the curse in my absent-minded state, for my friends warned me most earnestly to show my husband the ring.

Kashyapa. My daughter, you know the truth. Do not now give way to anger against your rightful husband. Remember:

> The curse it was that brought defeat and pain;
> The darkness flies; you are his queen again.
> Reflections are not seen in dusty glass,
> Which, cleaned, will mirror all the things that pass.

King. It is most true, holy one.

Kashyapa. My son, I hope you have greeted as he deserves the son whom Shakuntala has borne you, for whom I myself have performed the birth-rite and the other ceremonies.

King. Holy one, the hope of my race centres in him.

Kashyapa. Know then that his courage will make him emperor.

> Journeying over every sea,
> His car will travel easily;
> The seven islands of the earth
> Will bow before his matchless worth;
> Because wild beasts to him were tame,
> All-tamer was his common name;
> As Bharata he shall be known,
> For he will bear the world alone.

King. I anticipate everything from him, since you have performed the rites for him.

Aditi. Kanva also should be informed that his daughter's wishes are fulfilled. But Menaka is waiting upon me here and cannot be spared.

Shakuntala (*to herself*). The holy one has expressed my own desire.

Kashyapa. Kanva knows the whole matter through his divine insight. (*He reflects.*) Yet he should hear from us the pleasant tidings, how his daughter and her son have been received by her husband. Who waits without? (*Enter a pupil.*)

Pupil. I am here, holy one.

Kashyapa. Galava, fly through the air at once, carrying pleasant tidings from me to holy Kanva. Tell him how Durvasas' curse has come to an end, how Dushyanta recovered his memory, and has taken Shakuntala with her child to himself.

Pupil. Yes, holy one. (*Exit.*)

Kashyapa (*to the king*). My son, enter with child and wife the chariot of your friend Indra, and set out for your capital.

King. Yes, holy one.

Kashyapa. For now

> May Indra send abundant rain,
> Repaid by sacrificial gain;
> With aid long mutually given,
> Rule you on earth, and he in heaven.

King. Holy one, I will do my best.

Kashyapa. What more, my son, shall I do for you?

King. Can there be more than this? Yet may this prayer be fulfilled.

May kingship benefit the land,
And wisdom grow in scholars' band;
May Shiva see my faith on earth
And make me free of all rebirth.

(*Exeunt omnes.*)

THE STORY OF SHAKUNTALA

THE STORY OF SHAKUNTALA

In the first book of the vast epic poem *Mahabharata*, Kalidasa found the story of Shakuntala. The story has a natural place there, for Bharata, Shakuntala's son, is the eponymous ancestor of the princes who play the leading part in the epic.

With no little abbreviation of its epic breadth, the story runs as follows:—

THE EPIC TALE

Once that strong-armed king, with a mighty host of men and chariots, entered a thick wood. Then when the king had slain thousands of wild creatures, he entered another wood with his troops and his chariots, intent on pursuing a deer. And the king beheld a wonderful, beautiful hermitage on the bank of the sacred river Malini; on its bank was the beautiful hermitage of blessèd, high-souled Kanva, whither the great sages resorted. Then the king determined to enter, that he might see the great sage Kanva, rich in holiness. He laid aside the insignia of royalty and went on alone, but did not see the austere sage in the hermitage. Then, when he did not see the sage, and perceived that the hermitage was deserted, he cried aloud, "Who is here?" until the forest seemed to shriek. Hearing his cry, a maiden, lovely as Shri, came from the hermitage, wearing a hermit garb. "Welcome!" she said at once, greeting him, and smilingly added: "What may be done for you?" Then the king said to the sweet-voiced maid: "I have come to pay reverence to the holy sage Kanva. Where has the blessèd one gone, sweet girl? Tell me this, lovely maid."

Shakuntala said: "My blessèd father has gone from the hermitage to gather fruits. Wait a moment. You shall see him when he returns."

The king did not see the sage, but when the lovely girl of the fair hips and charming smile spoke to him, he saw that she was radiant in her beauty, yes, in her hard vows and self-restraint all youth and beauty, and he said to her:

"Who are you? Whose are you, lovely maiden? Why did you come to the forest? Whence are you, sweet girl, so lovely and so good? Your beauty stole my heart at the first glance. I wish to know you better. Answer me, sweet maid."

The maiden laughed when thus questioned by the king in the hermitage, and the words she spoke were very sweet: "O Dushyanta, I am known as blessèd Kanva's daughter, and he is austere, steadfast, wise, and of a lofty soul."

Dushyanta said: "But he is chaste, glorious maid, holy, honoured by the world. Though virtue should swerve from its course, he would not swerve from the hardness of his vow. How were you born his daughter, for you are beautiful? I am in great perplexity about this. Pray remove it."

[Shakuntala here explains how she is the child of a sage and a nymph, deserted at birth, cared for by birds (*shakuntas*), found and reared by Kanva, who gave her the name Shakuntala.]

Dushyanta said: "You are clearly a king's daughter, sweet maiden, as you say. Become my lovely wife. Tell me, what shall I do for you? Let all my kingdom be yours to-day. Become my wife, sweet maid."

Shakuntala said: "Promise me truly what I say to you in secret. The son that is born to me must be your heir. If you promise, Dushyanta, I will marry you."

"So be it," said the king without thinking, and added: "I will bring you too to my city, sweet-smiling girl."

So the king took the faultlessly graceful maiden by the hand and dwelt with her. And when he had bidden her be of good courage, he went forth, saying again and again: "I will send a complete army for you, and tell them to bring my sweet-smiling bride to my palace." When he had made this promise, the king went thoughtfully to find Kanva. "What will he do when he hears it, this holy, austere man?" he wondered, and still thinking, he went back to his capital.

Now the moment he was gone, Kanva came to the hermitage. And Shakuntala was ashamed and did not come to meet her father. But blessèd, austere Kanva had divine discernment. He discovered her, and seeing the matter with celestial vision, he was pleased and said: "What you have done, dear, to-day, forgetting me and meeting a man, this does not break the law. A man who loves may marry secretly the woman who loves him without a ceremony; and Dushyanta is virtuous and noble, the best of men. Since you have found a loving husband, Shakuntala, a noble son shall be born to you, mighty in the world."

Sweet Shakuntala gave birth to a boy of unmeasured prowess. His hands were marked with the wheel, and he quickly grew to be a glorious boy. As a six years' child in Kanva's hermitage he rode on the backs of lions, tigers, and boars near the hermitage, and tamed them, and ran about playing with them. Then those who lived in Kanva's hermitage gave him a name. "Let him be called All-tamer," they said: "for he tames everything."

But when the sage saw the boy and his more than human deeds, he said to Shakuntala: "It is time for him to be anointed crown prince." When he saw how strong the boy was, Kanva said to his pupils: "Quickly bring my Shakuntala and her son from my house to her husband's palace. A long abiding with their relatives is not proper for married women. It destroys their reputation, and their character, and their virtue; so take her without delay." "We will," said all the mighty men, and they set out with Shakuntala and her son for Gajasahvaya.

When Shakuntala drew near, she was recognised and invited to enter, and she said to the king: "This is your son, O King. You must anoint him crown prince, just as you promised before, when we met."

When the king heard her, although he remembered her, he said: "I do not remember. To whom do you belong, you wicked hermit-woman? I do not remember a union with you for virtue, love, and wealth.[1] Either go or stay, or do whatever you wish."

When he said this, the sweet hermit-girl half fainted from shame and grief, and stood stiff as a pillar. Her eyes darkened with passionate indignation; her lips quivered; she seemed to consume the king as she gazed at him with sidelong glances. Concealing her feelings and nerved by anger, she held in check the magic power that her ascetic

[1] The Hindu equivalent of "for better, for worse."

life had given her. She seemed to meditate a moment, overcome by grief and anger. She gazed at her husband, then spoke passionately: " O shameless king, although you know, why do you say, 'I do not know,' like any other ordinary man? "

Dushyanta said: " I do not know the son born of you, Shakuntala. Women are liars. Who will believe what you say? Are you not ashamed to say these incredible things, especially in my presence? You wicked hermit-woman, go! "

Shakuntala said: " O King, sacred is holy God, and sacred is a holy promise. Do not break your promise, O King. Let your love be sacred. If you cling to a lie, and will not believe, alas! I must go away; there is no union with a man like you. For even without you, Dushyanta, my son shall rule this foursquare earth adorned with kingly mountains."

When she had said so much to the king, Shakuntala started to go. But a bodiless voice from heaven said to Dushyanta: " Care for your son, Dushyanta. Do not despise Shakuntala. You are the boy's father. Shakuntala tells the truth."

When he heard the utterance of the gods, the king joyfully said to his chaplain and his ministers: " Hear the words of this heavenly messenger. If I had received my son simply because of her words, he would be suspected by the world, he would not be pure."

Then the king received his son gladly and joyfully. He kissed his head and embraced him lovingly. His wife also Dushyanta honoured, as justice required. And the king soothed her, and said: " This union which I had with you was hidden from the world. Therefore I hesitated, O Queen, in order to save your reputation. And as for the cruel words you said to me in an excess of passion, these I pardon you, my beautiful, great-eyed darling, because you love me."

Then King Dushyanta gave the name Bharata to Shakuntala's son, and had him anointed crown prince.

It is plain that this story contains the material for a good play; the very form of the epic tale is largely dramatic. It is also plain, in a large way, of what nature are the principal changes which a dramatist must introduce in the original. For while Shakuntala is charming in the epic story, the king is decidedly contemptible. Somehow or other, his face must be saved.

To effect this, Kalidasa has changed the old story in three important respects. In the first place, he introduces the curse of Durvasas, clouding the king's memory, and saving him from moral responsibility in his rejection of Shakuntala. That there may be an ultimate recovery of memory, the curse is so modified as to last only until the king shall see again the ring which he has given to his bride. To the Hindu, curse and modification are matters of frequent occurrence; and Kalidasa has so delicately managed the matter as not to shock even a modern and Western reader with a feeling of strong improbability. Even to us it seems a natural part of the divine cloud that envelops the drama, in no way obscuring human passion, but rather giving to human passion an unwonted largeness and universality.

In the second place, the poet makes Shakuntala undertake her journey to the palace before her son is born. Obviously, the king's character is thus made to appear in a better light, and a greater probability is given to the whole story.

The third change is a necessary consequence of the first; for without the curse, there could have been no separation, no ensuing remorse, and no reunion.

But these changes do not of themselves make a drama out of the epic tale. Large additions were also necessary, both of scenes and of characters. We find, indeed, that only acts one and five, with a part of act seven, rest upon the ancient text, while acts two, three, four, and six, with most of seven, are a creation of the poet. As might have been anticipated, the acts of the former group are more dramatic, while those of the latter contribute more of poetical charm. It is with these that scissors must be chiefly busy when the play—rather too long for continuous presentation as it stands—is performed on the stage.

In the epic there are but three characters—Dushyanta, Shakuntala, Kanva, with the small boy running about in the background. To these Kalidasa has added from the palace, from the hermitage, and from the Elysian region which is represented with vague precision in the last act.

The conventional clown plays a much smaller part in this play than in the others which Kalidasa wrote. He has also less humour. The real humorous relief is given by the fisherman and the three policemen in the opening scene of the sixth act. This, it may be remarked, is the only scene of rollicking humour in Kalidasa's writing.

The forest scenes are peopled with quiet hermit-folk. Far the most charming of these are Shakuntala's girl friends. The two are beautifully differentiated: Anusuya grave, sober; Priyamvada vivacious, saucy; yet wonderfully united in friendship and in devotion to Shakuntala, whom they feel to possess a deeper nature than theirs.

Kanva, the hermit-father, hardly required any change from the epic Kanva. It was a happy thought to place beside him the staid, motherly Gautami. The small boy in the last act has magically become an individual in Kalidasa's hands. In this act too are the creatures of a higher world, their majesty not rendered too precise.

Dushyanta has been saved by the poet from his epic shabbiness; it may be doubted whether more has been done. There is in him, as in some other Hindu heroes, a shade too much of the meditative to suit our ideal of more alert and ready manhood.

But all the other characters sink into insignificance beside the heroine. Shakuntala dominates the play. She is actually on the stage in five of the acts, and her spirit pervades the other two, the second and the sixth. Shakuntala has held captive the heart of India for fifteen hundred years, and wins the love of increasing thousands in the West; for so noble a union of sweetness with strength is one of the miracles of art.

> Though lovely women walk the world to-day
> By tens of thousands, there is none so fair
> In all that exhibition and display
> With her most perfect beauty to compare—

because it is a most perfect beauty of soul no less than of outward form. Her character grows under our very eyes. When we first meet her, she is a simple maiden, knowing no greater sorrow than the death of a favourite deer; when we bid her farewell, she has passed through happy love, the mother's joys and pains, most cruel humiliation and suspicion, and the reunion with her husband, proved at last not to have been unworthy. And each of these great experiences has been met with a courage and a sweetness to which no words can render justice.

Kalidasa has added much to the epic tale; yet his use of the original is remarkably minute. A list of the epic suggestions incorporated in his play is long. But it is worth making, in order to show how keen is the eye of genius. Thus the king lays aside the insignia of royalty upon entering the grove (Act I). Shakuntala appears in hermit garb, a dress of bark (Act I). The quaint derivation of the heroine's name from *shakunta* —bird—is used with wonderful skill in a passage (Act VII) which defies translation, as it involves a play on words. The king's anxiety to discover whether the maiden's father is of a caste that permits her to marry him is reproduced (Act I). The marriage without a ceremony is retained (Act IV), but robbed of all offence. Kanva's celestial vision, which made it unnecessary for his child to tell him of her union with the king, is introduced with great delicacy (Act IV). The curious formation of the boy's hand which indicated imperial birth adds to the king's suspense (Act VII). The boy's rough play with wild animals is made convincing (Act VII) and his very nickname All-tamer is preserved (Act VII). Kanva's worldly wisdom as to husband and wife dwelling together is reproduced (Act IV). No small part of the give-and-take between the king and Shakuntala is given (Act V), but with a new dignity.

Of the construction of the play I speak with diffidence. It seems admirable to me, the apparently undue length of some scenes hardly constituting a blemish, as it was probably intended to give the actors considerable latitude of choice and excision. Several versions of the text have been preserved; it is from the longer of the two more familiar ones that the translation in this volume has been made. In the warm discussion over this matter, certain technical arguments of some weight have been advanced in favour of this choice; there is also a more general consideration which seems to me of importance. I find it hard to believe that any lesser artist could pad such a masterpiece, and pad it all over, without making the fraud apparent on almost every page. The briefer version, on the other hand, might easily grow out of the longer, either as an acting text, or as a school-book.

We cannot take leave of Shakuntala in any better way than by quoting the passage[1] in which Lévi's imagination has conjured up "the memorable *première* when Shakuntala saw the light, in the presence of Vikramaditya and his court."

La fête du printemps approche; Ujjayinî, la ville aux riches marchands et la capitale intellectuelle de l'Inde, glorieuse et prospère sous un roi victorieux et sage, se prépare à célébrer la solennité avec une pompe digne de son opulence et de son goût. . . . L'auteur applaudi de Mâlavikâ . . . le poète dont le souple génie s'accommode sans effort au ton de l'épopée ou de l'élégie, Kâlidâsa vient d'achever une comédie héroïque annoncée comme un chef-d'œuvre par la voix de ses amis. . . . Le poète a ses comédiens, qu'il a éprouvés et dressés à sa manière avec Mâlavikâ. Les comédiens suivront leur poète familier, devenu leur maître et leur ami. . . . Leur solide instruction, leur goût épuré reconnaissent les qualités maîtresses de l'œuvre, l'habileté de l'intrigue, le juste équilibre des sentiments, la fraîcheur de l'imagination . . .

Vikramâditya entre, suivi des courtisans, et s'asseoit sur son trône; ses femmes restent à sa gauche; à sa droite les rois vassaux accourus pour rendre leurs hommages, les princes, les hauts fonctionnaires, les littérateurs et les savants, groupés autour de Varâha-mihira l'astrologue et d'Amarasiṃha le lexicographe . . .

Tout à coup, les deux jolies figurantes placées devant le rideau de la coulisse en écartent les plis, et Duḥṣanta, l'arc et les flèches à la main, paraît monté sur un char; son cocher tient les rênes; lancés à la poursuite d'une gazelle imaginaire, ils simulent par leurs gestes la rapidité de la course; leurs stances pittoresques et descriptives suggèrent à l'imagination un décor que la peinture serait impuissante à tracer. Ils approchent de l'ermitage; le roi descend à terre, congédie le cocher, les chevaux et le char, entend les voix des jeunes filles et se cache. Un mouvement de curiosité

[1] *Le Théâtre Indien*, pages 368-371. This is without competition the best work in which any part of the Sanskrit literature has been treated, combining erudition, imagination, and taste. The book is itself literature of a high order. The passage is unfortunately too long to be quoted entire.

agite les spectateurs; fille d'une Apsaras et création de Kâlidâsa, Çakuntalâ réunit tous les charmes; l'actrice saura-t-elle répondre à l'attente des connaisseurs et réaliser l'idéal? Elle paraît, vêtue d'une simple tunique d'écorce qui semble cacher ses formes et par un contraste habile les embellit encore; la ligne arrondie du visage, les yeux longs, d'un bleu sombre, langoureux, les seins opulents mal emprisonnés, les bras délicats laissent à deviner les beautés que le costume ascétique dérobe. Son attitude, ses gestes ravissent à la fois les regards et les cœurs; elle parle, et sa voix est un chant. La cour de Vikramâditya frémit d'une émotion sereine et profonde: un chef-d'œuvre nouveau vient d'entrer dans l'immortalité.

THE TWO MINOR DRAMAS

THE TWO MINOR DRAMAS

I.—"MALAVIKA AND AGNIMITRA"

Malavika and Agnimitra is the earliest of Kalidasa's three dramas, and probably his earliest work. This conclusion would be almost certain from the character of the play, but is put beyond doubt by the following speeches of the prologue:

Stage-director. The audience has asked us to present at this spring festival a drama called *Malavika and Agnimitra*, composed by Kalidasa. Let the music begin.

Assistant. No, no! Shall we neglect the works of such illustrious authors as Bhasa, Saumilla, and Kaviputra? Can the audience feel any respect for the work of a modern poet, a Kalidasa?

Stage-director. You are quite mistaken. Consider:

Not all is good that bears an ancient name,
Nor need we every modern poem blame:
Wise men approve the good, or new or old;
The foolish critic follows where he's told.

Assistant. The responsibility rests with you, sir.

There is irony in the fact that the works of the illustrious authors mentioned have perished, that we should hardly know of their existence were it not for the tribute of their modest, youthful rival. But Kalidasa could not read the future. We can imagine his feelings of mingled pride and fear when his early work was presented at the spring festival before the court of King Vikramaditya, without doubt the most polished and critical audience that could at that hour have been gathered in any city on earth.

The play which sought the approbation of this audience

shows no originality of plot, no depth of passion. It is a light, graceful drama of court intrigue. The hero, King Agnimitra, is an historical character of the second century before Christ, and Kalidasa's play gives us some information about him that history can seriously consider. The play represents Agnimitra's father, the founder of the Sunga dynasty, as still living. As the seat of empire was in Patna on the Ganges, and as Agnimitra's capital is Vidisha—the modern Bhilsa—it seems that he served as regent of certain provinces during his father's lifetime. The war with the King of Vidarbha seems to be an historical occurrence, and the fight with the Greek cavalry force is an echo of the struggle with Menander, in which the Hindus were ultimately victorious. It was natural for Kalidasa to lay the scene of his play in Bhilsa rather than in the far-distant Patna, for it is probable that many in the audience were acquainted with the former city. It is to Bhilsa that the poet refers again in *The Cloud-Messenger*, where these words are addressed to the cloud:

At thine approach, Dasharna land is blest
With hedgerows where gay buds are all aglow,
With village trees alive with many a nest
Abuilding by the old familiar crow,
With lingering swans, with ripe rose-apples' darker show.

There shalt thou see the royal city, known
Afar, and win the lover's fee complete,
If thou subdue thy thunders to a tone
Of murmurous gentleness, and taste the sweet,
Love-rippling features of the river at thy feet.

Yet in Kalidasa's day, the glories of the Sunga dynasty were long departed, nor can we see why the poet should have chosen his hero and his era as he did.

There follows an analysis of the plot and some slight criticism.

In addition to the stage-director and his assistant, who appear in the prologue, the characters of the play are these:

AGNIMITRA, *king in Vidisha.*
GAUTAMA, *a clown, his friend.*
GANADASA, HARADATTA } *dancing-masters.*
DHARINI, *the senior queen.*
IRAVATI, *the junior queen.*
MALAVIKA, *maid to Queen Dharini, later discovered to be a princess.*
KAUSHIKI, *a Buddhist nun.*
BAKULAVALIKA, *a maid, friend of Malavika.*
NIPUNIKA, *maid to Queen Iravati.*

A counsellor, a chamberlain, a humpback, two court poets, maids, and mute attendants.

The scene is the palace and gardens of King Agnimitra, the time a few days.

ACT I.—After the usual prologue, the maid Bakulavalika appears with another maid. From their conversation we learn that King Agnimitra has seen in the palace picture-gallery a new painting of Queen Dharini with her attendants. So beautiful is one of these, Malavika, that the king is smitten with love, but is prevented by the jealous queen from viewing the original. At this point the dancing-master Ganadasa enters. From him Bakulavalika learns that Malavika is a wonderfully proficient pupil, while he learns from her that Malavika had been sent as a present to Queen Dharini by a general commanding a border fortress, the queen's brother.

After this introductory scene, the king enters, and listens to a letter sent by the king of Vidarbha. The rival monarch had imprisoned a prince and princess, cousins of Agnimitra, and in response to Agnimitra's demand that they be set free, he declares that the princess has escaped, but that the prince shall not be liberated except on certain conditions. This letter so angers Agnimitra that he despatches an army against the king of Vidarbha.

Gautama, the clown, informs Agnimitra that he has devised a plan for bringing Malavika into the king's presence. He has stirred an envious rivalry in the bosoms of the two dancing-masters, who soon appear, each abusing the other vigorously, and claiming for himself the pre-eminence in their art. It is agreed that each shall exhibit his best pupil before the king, Queen Dharini, and the learned Buddhist nun, Kaushiki. The nun, who is in the secret of the king's desire, is made mistress of ceremonies, and the queen's jealous opposition is overborne.

Act II.—The scene is laid in the concert-hall of the palace. The nun determines that Ganadasa shall present his pupil first. Malavika is thereupon introduced, dances, and sings a song which pretty plainly indicates her own love for the king. He is in turn quite ravished, finding her far more beautiful even than the picture. The clown manages to detain her some little time by starting a discussion as to her art, and when she is finally permitted to depart, both she and the king are deeply in love. The court poet announces the noon hour, and the exhibition of the other dancing-master is postponed.

Act III.—The scene is laid in the palace garden. From the conversation of two maids it appears that a favourite ashoka-tree is late in blossoming. This kind of tree, so the belief runs, can be induced to put forth blossoms if touched by the foot of a beautiful woman in splendid garments.

When the girls depart, the king enters with the clown, his confidant. The clown, after listening to the king's lovelorn confidences, reminds him that he has agreed to meet his young Queen Iravati in the garden, and swing with her. But before the queen's arrival, Malavika enters, sent thither by Dharini to touch the ashoka-tree with her foot, and thus encourage it to blossom. The king and the clown hide in a thicket, to feast their eyes upon her. Presently the maid Bakulavalika appears, to adorn Malavika for the ceremony, and engages her in conversation about the king. But now a third pair enter, the young Queen Iravati, somewhat flushed with wine, and her maid Nipunika. They also conceal themselves to spy upon the young girls. Thus there are three groups upon the stage: the two girls believe themselves to be alone; the king and the clown are aware of the two girls, as are also the queen and her maid; but neither of these two pairs knows of the presence of the other. This situation gives rise to very entertaining dialogue, which changes its character when the king starts forward to express his love for Malavika. Another sudden change is brought about when Iravati, mad with jealousy, joins the group, sends the two girls away, and berates the king. He excuses himself as earnestly as a man may when caught in such a predicament, but cannot appease the young queen, who leaves him with words of bitter jealousy.

Act IV.—The clown informs the king that Queen Dharini has locked Malavika and her friend in the cellar, and has given orders to the doorkeeper that they are to be released only upon presentation of her own signet-ring, engraved with the figure of a serpent. But he declares that he has devised a plan to set them free. He bids the king wait upon Queen Dharini, and presently rushes into their presence, showing his thumb marked with two scratches, and declaring that he has been bitten by a cobra. Imploring the king to care for his childless mother, he awakens genuine sympathy in the queen, who readily parts with her serpent-ring, supposed to be efficacious in charming away the effects of snake-poison. Needless to say, he uses the ring to procure the freedom of Malavika and her friend, and then brings about a meeting with Agnimitra in the summer-house. The love-scene which follows is again interrupted by Queen Iravati. This time the king is saved by the news that his little daughter has been frightened by a yellow monkey, and will be comforted only by him. The act ends with the announcement that the ashoka-tree has blossomed.

Act V.—It now appears that Queen Dharini has relented and is willing to unite Malavika with the king; for she invites him to meet her under the ashoka-tree, and includes Malavika among her attendants. Word is brought that the army despatched against the king of Vidarbha has been completely successful, and that in the spoil are included two maids with remarkable powers of song. These maids are brought before the company gathered at the tree, where they surprise every one by falling on their faces before Malavika with the exclamation, "Our princess!" Here the Buddhist nun takes up the tale. She tells how her brother, the counsellor of the captive prince, had rescued her and Malavika from the king of Vidarbha, and had started for Agnimitra's court.

On the way they had been overpowered by robbers, her brother killed, and she herself separated from Malavika. She had thereupon become a nun and made her way to Agnimitra's court, and had there found Malavika, who had been taken from the robbers by Agnimitra's general and sent as a present to Queen Dharini. She had not divulged the matter sooner, because of a prophecy that Malavika should be a servant for just one year before becoming a king's bride. This recital removes any possible objection to a union of Malavika and Agnimitra. To complete the king's happiness, there comes a letter announcing that his son by Dharini has won a victory over a force of Greek cavalry, and inviting the court to be present at the sacrifice which was to follow the victory. Thus every one is made happy except the jealous young Queen Iravati, now to be supplanted by Malavika; yet even she consents, though somewhat ungraciously, to the arrangements made.

Criticism of the large outlines of this plot would be quite unjust, for it is completely conventional. In dozens of plays we have the same story: the king who falls in love with a maid-servant, the jealousy of his harem, the eventual discovery that the maid is of royal birth, and the addition of another wife to a number already sufficiently large. In writing a play of this kind, the poet frankly accepts the conventions; his ingenuity is shown in the minor incidents, in stanzas of poetical description, and in giving abundant opportunity for graceful music and dancing. When the play is approached in this way, it is easy to see the *griffe du lion* in this, the earliest work of the greatest poet who ever sang repeatedly of love between man and woman, troubled for a time but eventually happy. For though there is in Agnimitra, as in all heroes of his type, something contemptible, there is in Malavika a sweetness, a delicacy, a purity, that make her no unworthy precursor of Sita, of Indumati, of the Yaksha's bride, and of Shakuntala.

II.—"URVASHI"

The second of the two inferior dramas may be conveniently called *Urvashi*, though the full title is *The Tale of Urvashi won by Valour*. When and where the play was first produced we do not know, for the prologue is silent as to these matters. It has been thought that it was the last work of Kalidasa, even that it was never produced in his lifetime. Some support is lent to this theory by the fact that the play is filled with reminiscences of Shakuntala, in small matters as well as in great; as if the poet's imagination had grown weary, and he were willing to repeat himself. Yet *Urvashi* is a much more ambitious effort than *Malavika*, and invites a fuller criticism, after an outline of the plot has been given.

In addition to the stage-director and his assistant, who appear in the prologue, the characters of the play are these:

PURURAVAS, *king in Pratishthana on the Ganges.*
AYUS, *his son.*
MANAVAKA, *a clown, his friend.*
URVASHI, *a heavenly nymph.*
CHITRALEKHA, *another nymph, her friend.*
AUSHINARI, *queen of Pururavas.*
NIPUNIKA, *her maid.*

A charioteer, a chamberlain, a hermit-woman, various nymphs and other divine beings, and attendants.

The scene shifts as indicated in the following analysis. The time of the first four acts is a few days. Between acts four and five several years elapse.

ACT I.—The prologue only tells us that we may expect a new play of Kalidasa. A company of heavenly nymphs then appear upon Mount Gold-peak wailing and calling for help. Their cries are answered by King Pururavas, who rides in a chariot that flies through the air. In response to his inquiries, the nymphs inform him that two of their number, Urvashi and Chitralekha, have been carried into captivity by a demon. The king darts in pursuit, and presently returns, victorious, with the two nymphs. As soon as Urvashi recovers consciousness, and has rejoined her joyful friends, it is made plain that she and the king have been deeply impressed with each other's attractions. The king is compelled to decline an invitation to visit Paradise, but he and Urvashi exchange loving glances before they part.

Act II.—The act opens with a comic scene in the king's palace. The clown appears, bursting with the secret of the king's love for Urvashi, which has been confided to him. He is joined by the maid Nipunika, commissioned by the queen to discover what it is that occupies the king's mind. She discovers the secret ingeniously, but without much difficulty, and gleefully departs.

The king and the clown then appear in the garden, and the king expresses at some length the depth and seeming hopelessness of his passion. The latter part of his lament is overheard by Urvashi herself, who, impelled by love for the king, has come down to earth with her friend Chitralekha, and now stands near, listening but invisible. When she has heard enough to satisfy her of the king's passion, she writes a love-stanza on a birch-leaf, and lets it fall before him. His reception of this token is such that Urvashi throws aside the magic veil that renders her invisible, but as soon as she has greeted the king, she and her friend are called away to take their parts in a play that is being presented in Paradise.

The king and the clown hunt for Urvashi's love-letter, which has been neglected during the past few minutes. But the leaf has blown away, only to be picked up and read by Nipunika, who at that moment enters with the queen. The queen can hardly be deceived by the lame excuses which the king makes, and after offering her ironical congratulations, jealously leaves him.

Act III.—The act opens with a conversation between two minor personages in Paradise. It appears that Urvashi had taken the heroine's part in the drama just presented there, and when asked, "On whom is your heart set?" had absent-mindedly replied, "On Pururavas." Heaven's stage-director had thereupon cursed her to fall from Paradise, but this curse had been thus modified: that she was to live on earth with Pururavas until he should see a child born of her, and was then to return.

The scene shifts to Pururavas' palace. In the early evening, the chamberlain brings the king a message, inviting him to meet the queen on a balcony bathed in the light of the rising moon. The king betakes himself thither with his friend, the clown. In the midst of a dialogue concerning moonlight and love, Urvashi and Chitralekha enter from Paradise, wearing as before veils of invisibility. Presently the queen appears and with humble dignity asks pardon of the king for her rudeness, adding that she will welcome any new queen whom he genuinely loves and who genuinely returns his love. When the queen departs, Urvashi creeps up behind the king and puts her hands over his eyes. Chitralekha departs after begging the king to make her friend forget Paradise.

Act IV.—From a short dialogue in Paradise between Chitralekha and another nymph, we learn that a misfortune has befallen Pururavas and Urvashi. During their honeymoon in a delightful Himalayan forest, Urvashi, in a fit of jealousy, had left her husband, and had inadvertently entered a grove forbidden by an austere god to women. She was straightway transformed into a vine, while Pururavas is wandering through the forest in desolate anguish.

The scene of what follows is laid in the Himalayan forest. Pururavas enters, and in a long poetical soliloquy bewails his loss and seeks for traces of Urvashi. He vainly asks help of the creatures whom he meets: a peacock, a cuckoo, a swan, a ruddy goose, a bee, an elephant, a mountain-echo, a river, and an antelope. At last he finds a brilliant ruby in a cleft of the rocks, and when about to throw it away, is told by a hermit to preserve it: for this is the gem of reunion, and one who possesses it will soon be reunited with his love. With the gem in his hand, Pururavas comes to a vine which mysteriously reminds him of Urvashi, and when he embraces it, he finds his belovèd in his arms. After she has explained to him the reason of her transformation, they determine to return to the king's capital.

ACT V.—The scene of the concluding act is the king's palace. Several years have passed in happy love, and Pururavas has only one sorrow—that he is childless.

One day a vulture snatches from a maid's hand the treasured gem of reunion, which he takes to be a bit of bloody meat, and flies off with it, escaping before he can be killed. While the king and his companions lament the gem's loss, the chamberlain enters, bringing the gem and an arrow with which the bird had been shot. On the arrow is written a verse declaring it to be the property of Ayus, son of Pururavas and Urvashi. A hermit-woman is then ushered in, who brings a lad with her. She explains that the lad had been entrusted to her as soon as born by Urvashi, and that it was he who had just shot the bird and recovered the gem. When Urvashi is summoned to explain why she had concealed her child, she reminds the king of heaven's decree that she should return as soon as Pururavas should see the child to be born to them. She had therefore sacrificed maternal love to conjugal affection. Upon this, the king's new-found joy gives way to gloom. He determines to give up his kingdom and spend the remainder of his life as a hermit in the forest. But the situation is saved by a messenger from Paradise, bearing heaven's decree that Urvashi shall live with the king until his death. A troop of nymphs then enter and assist in the solemn consecration of Ayus as crown prince.

The tale of Pururavas and Urvashi, which Kalidasa has treated dramatically, is first made known to us in the Rigveda. It is thus one of the few tales that so caught the Hindu imagination as to survive the profound change which came over Indian thinking in the passage from Vedic to classical times. As might be expected from its history, it is told in many widely differing forms, of which the oldest and best may be summarised thus.

Pururavas, a mortal, sees and loves the nymph Urvashi. She consents to live with him on earth so long as he shall not break certain trivial conditions. Some time after the birth of a son, these conditions are broken, through no fault of the man, and she leaves him. He wanders disconsolate, finds her, and pleads with her, by her duty as a wife, by her love for her child, even by a threat of suicide. She rejects his entreaties, declaring that there can be no lasting love between mortal and immortal, even adding: "There are no friendships with women. Their hearts are the hearts of hyenas." Though at last she comforts him with vague hopes of a future happiness, the story remains, as indeed it must remain, a tragedy—the tragedy of love between human and divine.

This splendid tragic story Kalidasa has ruined. He has made of it an ordinary tale of domestic intrigue, has changed the nymph of heaven into a member of an earthly harem. The more important changes made by Kalidasa in the traditional story, all have the tendency to remove the massive, godlike, austere features of the tale, and to substitute something graceful or even pretty. These principal changes are: the introduction of the queen, the clown, and the whole human paraphernalia of a court; the curse pronounced on Urvashi for her carelessness in the heavenly drama, and its modification; the invention of the gem of reunion; and the final removal of the curse, even as modified. It is true that the Indian theatre permits no tragedy, and we may well believe that no successor of Kalidasa could hope to present a tragedy on the stage. But might not Kalidasa, far overtopping his predecessors, have put on the stage a drama the story of which was already familiar to his audience as a tragic story? Perhaps not. If not, one can but wish that he had chosen another subject.

This violent twisting of an essentially tragic story has had a further ill consequence in weakening the individual characters. Pururavas is a mere conventional hero, in no way different from fifty others, in spite of his divine lineage and his successful wooing of a goddess. Urvashi is too much of a nymph to be a woman, and too much of a woman to be a nymph. The other characters are mere types.

Yet, in spite of these obvious objections, Hindu critical opinion has always rated the *Urvashi* very high, and I have long hesitated to make adverse comments upon it, for it is surely true that every nation is the best judge of its own literature. And indeed, if one could but forget plot and characters, he would find in *Urvashi* much to attract and charm. There is no lack of humour in the clever maid who worms the clown's secret out of him. There is no lack of a certain shrewdness in the clown, as when he observes:

"Who wants heaven? It is nothing to eat or drink. It is just a place where they never shut their eyes—like fishes!"

Again, the play offers an opportunity for charming scenic display. The terrified nymphs gathered on the mountain, the palace balcony bathed in moonlight, the forest through which the king wanders in search of his lost darling, the concluding solemn consecration of the crown prince by heavenly beings—these scenes show that Kalidasa was no closet dramatist. And finally, there is here and there such poetry as only Kalidasa could write. The fourth act particularly, undramatic as it is, is full of a delicate beauty that defies transcription. It was a new and daring thought—to present on the stage a long lyrical monologue addressed to the creatures of the forest and inspired by despairing passion. Nor must it be forgotten that this play, like all Indian plays, is an opera. The music and the dancing are lost. We judge it perforce unfairly, for we judge it by the text alone. If, in spite of all, the *Urvashi* is a failure, it is a failure possible only to a serene and mighty poet.

THE DYNASTY OF RAGHU

THE DYNASTY OF RAGHU

The Dynasty of Raghu is an epic poem in nineteen cantos. It consists of 1564 stanzas, or something over six thousand lines of verse. The subject is that great line of kings who traced their origin to the sun, the famous "solar line" of Indian story. The bright particular star of the solar line is Rama, the knight without fear and without reproach, the Indian ideal of a gentleman. His story had been told long before Kalidasa's time in the *Ramayana*, an epic which does not need to shun comparison with the foremost epic poems of Europe. In *The Dynasty of Raghu*, too, Rama is the central figure; yet in Kalidasa's poem there is much detail concerning other princes of the line. The poem thus naturally falls into three great parts: first, the four immediate ancestors of Rama (cantos 1-9); second, Rama (cantos 10-15); third, certain descendants of Rama (cantos 16-19). A somewhat detailed account of the matter of the poem may well precede criticism and comment.

First canto. The journey to the hermitage.—The poem begins with the customary brief prayer for Shiva's favour:

God Shiva and his mountain bride,
Like word and meaning unified,
The world's great parents, I beseech
To join fit meaning to my speech.

Then follow nine stanzas in which Kalidasa speaks more directly of himself than elsewhere in his works:

How great is Raghu's solar line!
How feebly small are powers of mine!
As if upon the ocean's swell
I launched a puny cockle-shell.

The fool who seeks a poet's fame
Must look for ridicule and blame,
Like tiptoe dwarf who fain would try
To pluck the fruit for giants high.

Yet I may enter through the door
That mightier poets pierced of yore;
A thread may pierce a jewel, but
Must follow where the diamond cut.

Of kings who lived as saints from birth,
Who ruled to ocean-shore on earth,
Who toiled until success was given,
Whose chariots stormed the gates of heaven,

Whose pious offerings were blest,
Who gave his wish to every guest,
Whose punishments were as the crimes,
Who woke to guard the world betimes,

Who sought, that they might lavish, pelf,
Whose measured speech was truth itself,
Who fought victorious wars for fame,
Who loved in wives the mother's name,

Who studied all good arts as boys,
Who loved, in manhood, manhood's joys,
Whose age was free from worldly care,
Who breathed their lives away in prayer,

Of these I sing, of Raghu's line,
Though weak mine art, and wisdom mine.
Forgive these idle stammerings
And think: For virtue's sake he sings.

The good who hear me will be glad
To pluck the good from out the bad;
When ore is proved by fire, the loss
Is not of purest gold, but dross.

After the briefest glance at the origin of the solar line, the poet tells of Rama's great-great-grandfather, King Dilipa. The detailed description of Dilipa's virtues has interest as showing Kalidasa's ideal of an aristocrat; a brief sample must suffice here:

He practised virtue, though in health;
Won riches, with no greed for wealth;
Guarded his life, though not from fear;
Prized joys of earth, but not too dear.

His virtuous foes he could esteem
Like bitter drugs that healing seem;
The friends who sinned he could forsake
Like fingers bitten by a snake.

Yet King Dilipa has one deep-seated grief: he has no son. He therefore journeys with his queen to the hermitage of the sage Vasishtha, in order to learn what they must do to propitiate an offended fate. Their chariot rolls over country roads past fragrant lotus-ponds and screaming peacocks and trustful deer, under archways formed without supporting pillars by the cranes, through villages where they receive the blessings of the people. At sunset they reach the peaceful forest hermitage, and are welcomed by the sage. In response to Vasishtha's benevolent inquiries, the king declares that all goes well in the kingdom, and yet:

Until from this dear wife there springs
A son as great as former kings,
The seven islands of the earth
And all their gems, are nothing worth.

The final debt, most holy one,
Which still I owe to life—a son—
Galls me as galls the cutting chain
An elephant housed in dirt and pain.

Vasishtha tells the king that on a former occasion he had offended the divine cow Fragrant, and had been cursed by the cow to lack children until he had propitiated her own offspring. While the sage is speaking, Fragrant's daughter approaches, and is entrusted to the care of the king and queen.

Second canto. The holy cow's gift.—During twenty-one days the king accompanies the cow during her wanderings in the forest, and each night the queen welcomes their return to the hermitage. On the twenty-second day the cow is attacked by a lion, and when the king hastens to draw an arrow, his arm is magically numbed, so that he stands helpless. To increase his horror, the lion speaks with a human voice, saying that he is a servant of the god Shiva, set on guard there and eating as his appointed food any animals that may appear. Dilipa perceives that a struggle with earthly weapons is useless, and begs the lion to accept his own body as the price of the cow's release. The lion tries sophistry, using the old, hollow arguments:

Great beauty and fresh youth are yours; on earth
As sole, unrivalled emperor you rule;
Should you redeem a thing of little worth
At such a price, you would appear a fool.

If pity moves you, think that one mere cow
Would be the gainer, should you choose to die;
Live rather for the world! Remember how
The father-king can bid all dangers fly.

And if the fiery sage's wrath, aglow
At loss of one sole cow, should make you shudder,
Appease his anger; for you can bestow
Cows by the million, each with pot-like udder.

Save life and youth; for to the dead are given
No long, unbroken years of joyous mirth;
But riches and imperial power are heaven—
The gods have nothing that you lack on earth.

The lion spoke and ceased; but echo rolled
Forth from the caves wherein the sound was pent,
As if the hills applauded manifold,
Repeating once again the argument.

Dilipa has no trouble in piercing this sophistical argument, and again offers his own life, begging the lion to spare the body of his fame rather than the body of his flesh. The lion consents, but when the king resolutely presents himself to be eaten, the illusion vanishes, and the holy cow grants the king his desire. The king returns to his capital with the queen, who shortly becomes pregnant.

Third canto. Raghu's consecration.—The queen gives birth to a glorious boy, whom the joyful father names Raghu. There follows a description of the happy family, of which a few stanzas are given here:

The king drank pleasure from him late and soon
With eyes that stared like windless lotus-flowers;
Unselfish joy expanded all his powers
As swells the sea responsive to the moon.

The rooted love that filled each parent's soul
For the other, deep as bird's love for the mate,
Was now divided with the boy; and straight
The remaining half proved greater than the whole.

He learned the reverence that befits a boy;
Following the nurse's words, began to talk;
And clinging to her finger, learned to walk:
These childish lessons stretched his father's joy,

Who clasped the baby to his breast, and thrilled
To feel the nectar-touch upon his skin,
Half closed his eyes, the father's bliss to win
Which, more for long delay, his being filled.

The baby hair must needs be clipped; yet he
Retained two dangling locks, his cheeks to fret;
And down the river of the alphabet
He swam, with other boys, to learning's sea.

Religion's rites, and what good learning suits
A prince, he had from teachers old and wise;
Not theirs the pain of barren enterprise,
For effort spent on good material, fruits.

This happy childhood is followed by a youth equally happy. Raghu is married and made crown prince. He is entrusted with the care of the horse of sacrifice,[1] and when Indra, king of the gods, steals the horse, Raghu fights him. He cannot overcome the king of heaven, yet he acquits himself so creditably that he wins Indra's friendship. In consequence of this proof of his manhood, the empire is bestowed upon Raghu by his father, who retires with his queen to the forest, to spend his last days and prepare for death.

Fourth canto. Raghu conquers the world.—The canto opens with several stanzas descriptive of the glory of youthful King Raghu.

He manifested royal worth
By even justice toward the earth,
Beloved as is the southern breeze,
Too cool to burn, too warm to freeze.

The people loved his father, yet
For greater virtues could forget;
The beauty of the blossoms fair
Is lost when mango-fruits are there.

But the vassal kings are restless

For when they knew the king was gone
And power was wielded by his son,
The wrath of subject kings awoke,
Which had been damped in sullen smoke.

Raghu therefore determines to make a warlike progress through all India. He marches eastward with his army from his capital Ayodhya (the name is preserved in the modern

[1] If a king aspired to the title of emperor, or king of kings, he was at liberty to celebrate the horse-sacrifice. A horse was set free to wander at will for a year, and was escorted by a band of noble youths who were not permitted to interfere with his movements. If the horse wandered into the territory of another king, such king must either submit to be the vassal of the horse's owner, or must fight him. If the owner of the horse received the submission, with or without fighting, of all the kings into whose territories the horse wandered during the year of freedom, he offered the horse in sacrifice and assumed the imperial title.

Oudh) to the Bay of Bengal, then south along the eastern shore of India to Cape Comorin, then north along the western shore until he comes to the region drained by the Indus, finally east through the tremendous Himalaya range into Assam, and thence home. The various nations whom he encounters, Hindus, Persians, Greeks, and White Huns, all submit either with or without fighting. On his safe return, Raghu offers a great sacrifice and gives away all his wealth.[1]

Fifth canto. Aja goes wooing.—While King Raghu is penniless, a young sage comes to him, desiring a huge sum of money to give to the teacher with whom he has just finished his education. The king, unwilling that any suppliant should go away unsatisfied, prepares to assail the god of wealth in his Himalayan stronghold, and the god, rather than risk the combat, sends a rain of gold into the king's treasury. This gold King Raghu bestows upon the sage, who gratefully uses his spiritual power to cause a son to be born to his benefactor. In course of time, the son is born and the name Aja is given to him. We are here introduced to Prince Aja, who is a kind of secondary hero in the poem, inferior only to his mighty grandson, Rama. To Aja are devoted the remainder of this fifth canto and the following three cantos; and these Aja-cantos are among the loveliest in the epic. When the prince has grown into young manhood, he journeys to a neighbouring court to participate in the marriage reception of Princess Indumati.[2] One evening he camps by a river, from which a wild elephant issues and attacks his party. When wounded by Aja, the elephant strangely changes his form, becoming a demigod, gives the prince a magic weapon, and departs to heaven. Aja pro-

[1] This is not the place to discuss the many interesting questions of geography and ethnology suggested by the fourth canto. But it is important to notice that Kalidasa had at least superficial knowledge of the entire Indian peninsula and of certain outlying regions.

[2] A girl of the warrior caste had the privilege of choosing her husband. The procedure was this. All the eligible youths of the neighbourhood were invited to her house, and were lavishly entertained. On the appointed day, they assembled in a hall of the palace, and the maiden entered with a garland in her hand. The suitors were presented to her with some account of their claims upon her attention, after which she threw the garland around the neck of him whom she preferred.

ceeds without further adventure to the country and the palace of Princess Indumati, where he is made welcome and luxuriously lodged for the night. In the morning, he is awakened by the song of the court poets outside his chamber. He rises and betakes himself to the hall where the suitors are gathering.

Sixth canto. The princess chooses.—The princely suitors assemble in the hall; then, to the sound of music, the princess enters in a litter, robed as a bride, and creates a profound sensation.

For when they saw God's masterpiece, the maid
  Who smote their eyes to other objects blind,
Their glances, wishes, hearts, in homage paid,
  Flew forth to her; mere flesh remained behind.

The princes could not but betray their yearning
  By sending messengers, their love to bring,
In many a quick, involuntary turning,
  As flowering twigs of trees announce the spring.

Then a maid-servant conducts the princess from one suitor to another, and explains the claim which each has upon her affection. First is presented the King of Magadha, recommended in four stanzas, one of which runs:

Though other kings by thousands numbered be,
  He seems the one, sole governor of earth;
Stars, constellations, planets, fade and flee
  When to the moon the night has given birth.

But the princess is not attracted.

The slender maiden glanced at him; she glanced
  And uttered not a word, nor heeded how
The grass-twined blossoms of her garland danced
  When she dismissed him with a formal bow.

They pass to the next candidate, the king of the Anga country, in whose behalf this, and more, is said:

Learning and wealth by nature are at strife,
  Yet dwell at peace in him; and for the two
You would be fit companion as his wife,
  Like wealth enticing, and like learning true.

Him too the princess rejects, " not that he was unworthy of love, or she lacking in discernment, but tastes differ." She is then conducted to the King of Avanti:

And if this youthful prince your fancy pleases,
  Bewitching maiden, you and he may play
In those unmeasured gardens that the breezes
  From Sipra's billows ruffle, cool with spray.

The inducement is insufficient, and a new candidate is presented, the King of Anupa,

A prince whose fathers' glories cannot fade,
  By whom the love of learned men is wooed,
Who proves that Fortune is no fickle jade
  When he she chooses is not fickly good.

But alas!

She saw that he was brave to look upon,
  Yet could not feel his love would make her gay;
Full moons of autumn nights, when clouds are gone,
  Tempt not the lotus-flowers that bloom by day.

The King of Shurasena has no better fortune, in spite of his virtues and his wealth. As a river hurrying to the sea passes by a mountain that would detain her, so the princess passes him by. She is next introduced to the king of the Kalinga country;

His palace overlooks the ocean dark
  With windows gazing on the unresting deep,
Whose gentle thunders drown the drums that mark
  The hours of night, and wake him from his sleep.

But the maiden can no more feel at home with him than the

goddess of fortune can with a good but unlucky man. She therefore turns her attention to the king of the Pandya country in far southern India. But she is unmoved by hearing of the magic charm of the south, and rejects him too.

And every prince rejected while she sought
  A husband, darkly frowned, as turrets, bright
One moment with the flame from torches caught,
  Frown gloomily again and sink in night.

The princess then approaches Aja, who trembles lest she pass him by, as she has passed by the other suitors. The maid who accompanies Indumati sees that Aja awakens a deeper feeling, and she therefore gives a longer account of his kingly line, ending with the recommendation:

High lineage is his, fresh beauty, youth,
  And virtue shaped in kingly breeding's mould;
Choose him, for he is worth your love; in truth,
  A gem is ever fitly set in gold.

The princess looks lovingly at the handsome youth, but cannot speak for modesty. She is made to understand her own feelings when the maid invites her to pass on to the next candidate. Then the wreath is placed round Aja's neck, the people of the city shout their approval, and the disappointed suitors feel like night-blooming lotuses at daybreak.

Seventh canto. Aja's marriage.—While the suitors retire to the camps where they have left their retainers, Aja conducts Indumati into the decorated and festive city. The windows are filled with the faces of eager and excited women, who admire the beauty of the young prince and the wisdom of the princess's choice. When the marriage ceremony has been happily celebrated, the disappointed suitors say farewell with pleasant faces and jealous hearts, like peaceful pools concealing crocodiles. They lie in ambush on the road which he must take, and when he passes with his young bride, they fall upon him. Aja provides for the safety of Indumati, marshals his attendants, and greatly distinguishes himself in the battle which follows. Finally he uses the magic weapon, given him by the demigod, to benumb his adversaries, and leaving them in this helpless condition, returns home. He and his young bride are joyfully welcomed by King Raghu, who resigns the kingdom in favour of Aja.

Eighth canto. Aja's lament.—As soon as King Aja is firmly established on his throne, Raghu retires to a hermitage to prepare for the death of his mortal part. After some years of religious meditation he is released, attaining union with the eternal spirit which is beyond all darkness. His obsequies are performed by his dutiful son. Indumati gives birth to a splendid boy, who is named Dasharatha. One day, as the queen is playing with her husband in the garden, a wreath of magic flowers falls upon her from heaven, and she dies. The stricken king clasps the body of his dead belovèd, and laments over her.

If flowers that hardly touch the body, slay it,
The simplest instruments of fate may bring
Destruction, and we have no power to stay it;
Then must we live in fear of everything?

No! Death was right. He spared the sterner anguish;
Through gentle flowers your gentle life was lost
As I have seen the lotus fade and languish
When smitten by the slow and silent frost.

Yet God is hard. With unforgiving rigour
He forged a bolt to crush this heart of mine;
He left the sturdy tree its living vigour,
But stripped away and slew the clinging vine.

Through all the years, dear, you would not reprove me,
Though I offended. Can you go away
Sudden, without a word? I know you love me,
And I have not offended you to-day.

You surely thought me faithless, to be banished
As light-of-love and gambler, from your life,
Because without a farewell word, you vanished
And never will return, sweet-smiling wife.

The warmth and blush that followed after kisses
  Is still upon her face, to madden me;
For life is gone, 'tis only life she misses.
  A curse upon such life's uncertainty!

I never wronged you with a thought unspoken,
  Still less with actions. Whither are you flown?
Though king in name, I am a man heartbroken,
  For power and love took root in you alone.

Your bee-black hair from which the flowers are peeping,
  Dear, wavy hair that I have loved so well,
Stirs in the wind until I think you sleeping,
  Soon to return and make my glad heart swell.

Awake, my love! Let only life be given,
  And choking griefs that stifle now, will flee
As darkness from the mountain-cave is driven
  By magic herbs that glitter brilliantly.

The silent face, round which the curls are keeping
  Their scattered watch, is sad to look upon
As in the night some lonely lily, sleeping
  When musically humming bees are gone.

The girdle that from girlhood has befriended
  You, in love-secrets wise, discreet, and true,
No longer tinkles, now your dance is ended,
  Faithful in life, in dying faithful too.

Your low, sweet voice to nightingales was given;
  Your idly graceful movement to the swans;
Your grace to fluttering vines, dear wife in heaven;
  Your trustful, wide-eyed glances to the fawns:

You left your charms on earth, that I, reminded
  By them, might be consoled though you depart;
But vainly! Far from you, by sorrow blinded,
  I find no prop of comfort for my heart.

Remember how you planned to make a wedding,
  Giving the vine-bride to her mango-tree;

Before that happy day, dear, you are treading
The path with no return. It should not be.

And this ashoka-tree that you have tended
With eager longing for the blossoms red—
How can I twine the flowers that should have blended
With living curls, in garlands for the dead?

The tree remembers how the anklets, tinkling
On graceful feet, delighted other years;
Sad now he droops, your form with sorrow sprinkling,
And sheds his blossoms in a rain of tears.

Joy's sun is down, all love is fallen and perished,
The song of life is sung, the spring is dead,
Gone is the use of gems that once you cherished,
And empty, ever empty, is my bed.

You were my comrade gay, my home, my treasure,
You were my bosom's friend, in all things true,
My best-loved pupil in the arts of pleasure:
Stern death took all I had in taking you.

Still am I king, and rich in kingly fashion,
Yet lacking you, am poor the long years through;
I cannot now be won to any passion,
For all my passions centred, dear, in you.

Aja commits the body of his beloved queen to the flames. A holy hermit comes to tell the king that his wife had been a nymph of heaven in a former existence, and that she has now returned to her home. But Aja cannot be comforted. He lives eight weary years for the sake of his young son, then is reunited with his queen in Paradise.

Ninth canto. The hunt.—This canto introduces us to King Dasharatha, father of the heroic Rama. It begins with an elaborate description of his glory, justice, prowess, and piety; then tells of the three princesses who became his wives: Kausalya, Kaikeyi, and Sumitra. In the beautiful springtime he takes an extended hunting-trip in the forest, during which an accident happens, big with fate.

He left his soldiers far behind one day
In the wood, and following where deer-tracks lay,
Came with his weary horse adrip with foam
To river-banks where hermits made their home.

And in the stream he heard the water fill
A jar; he heard it ripple clear and shrill,
And shot an arrow, thinking he had found
A trumpeting elephant, toward the gurgling sound

Such actions are forbidden to a king,
Yet Dasharatha sinned and did this thing;
For even the wise and learned man is minded
To go astray, by selfish passion blinded.

He heard the startling cry, " My father! " rise
Among the reeds; rode up; before his eyes
He saw the jar, the wounded hermit boy:
Remorse transfixed his heart and killed his joy.

He left his horse, this monarch famous far,
Asked him who drooped upon the water-jar
His name, and from the stumbling accents knew
A hermit youth, of lowly birth but true.

The arrow still undrawn, the monarch bore
Him to his parents who, afflicted sore
With blindness, could not see their only son
Dying, and told them what his hand had done.

The murderer then obeyed their sad behest
And drew the fixèd arrow from his breast;
The boy lay dead; the father cursed the king,
With tear-stained hands, to equal suffering.

" In sorrow for your son you too shall die,
An old, old man," he said, " as sad as I."
Poor, trodden snake! He used his venomous sting,
Then heard the answer of the guilty king:

" Your curse is half a blessing if I see
The longed-for son who shall be born to me:

The scorching fire that sweeps the well-ploughed field,
May burn indeed, but stimulates the yield.

The deed is done; what kindly act can I
Perform who, pitiless, deserve to die?"
"Bring wood," he begged, "and build a funeral pyre,
That we may seek our son through death by fire."

The king fulfilled their wish; and while they burned,
In mute, sin-stricken sorrow he returned,
Hiding death's seed within him, as the sea
Hides magic fire that burns eternally.

Thus is foreshadowed the birth of Rama, his banishment, and the death of his father.

Cantos ten to fifteen form the kernel of the epic, for they tell the story of Rama, the mighty hero of Raghu's line. In these cantos Kalidasa attempts to present anew, with all the literary devices of a more sophisticated age, the famous old epic story sung in masterly fashion by the author of the *Ramayana*. As the poet is treading ground familiar to all who hear him, the action of these cantos is very compressed.

Tenth canto. The incarnation of Rama.—While Dasharatha, desiring a son, is childless, the gods, oppressed by a giant adversary, betake themselves to Vishnu, seeking aid. They sing a hymn of praise, a part of which is given here.

O thou who didst create this All,
Who dost preserve it, lest it fall,
Who wilt destroy it and its ways—
To thee, O triune Lord, be praise.

As into heaven's water run
The tastes of earth—yet it is one,
So thou art all the things that range
The universe, yet dost not change.

Far, far removed, yet ever near;
Untouched by passion, yet austere;

Sinless, yet pitiful of heart;
Ancient, yet free from age—Thou art.

Though uncreate, thou seekest birth;
Dreaming, thou watchest heaven and earth;
Passionless, smitest low thy foes;
Who knows thy nature, Lord? Who knows?

Though many different paths, O Lord,
May lead us to some great reward,
They gather and are merged in thee
Like floods of Ganges in the sea.

The saints who give thee every thought,
Whose every act for thee is wrought,
Yearn for thine everlasting peace,
For bliss with thee, that cannot cease.

Like pearls that grow in ocean's night,
Like sunbeams radiantly bright,
Thy strange and wonder-working ways
Defeat extravagance of praise.

If songs that to thy glory tend
Should weary grow or take an end,
Our impotence must bear the blame,
And not thine unexhausted name.

Vishnu is gratified by the praise of the gods, and asks their desire. They inform him that they are distressed by Ravana, the giant king of Lanka (Ceylon), whom they cannot conquer. Vishnu promises to aid them by descending to earth in a new avatar, as son of Dasharatha. Shortly afterwards, an angel appears before King Dasharatha, bringing in a golden bowl a substance which contains the essence of Vishnu. The king gives it to his three wives, who thereupon conceive and dream wonderful dreams. Then Queen Kausalya gives birth to Rama; Queen Kaikeyi to Bharata; Queen Sumitra to twins, Lakshmana and Shatrughna. Heaven and earth rejoice. The four princes grow up in mutual friendship, yet Rama and Lakshmana are peculiarly drawn to each other, as are Bharata and Shatrughna. So beautiful and so modest are the four boys that they seem like incarnations of the four things worth living for—virtue, money, love, and salvation.

Eleventh canto. The victory over Rama-with-the-axe.—At the request of the holy hermit Vishvamitra, the two youths Rama and Lakshmana visit his hermitage, to protect it from evil spirits. The two lads little suspect, on their maiden journey, how much of their lives will be spent in wandering together in the forest. On the way they are attacked by a giantess, whom Rama kills; the first of many giants who are to fall at his hand. He is given magic weapons by the hermit, with which he and his brother kill other giants, freeing the hermitage from all annoyance. The two brothers then travel with the hermit to the city of Mithila, attracted thither by hearing of its king, his wonderful daughter, and his wonderful bow. The bow was given him by the god Shiva; no man has been able to bend it; and the beautiful princess's hand is the prize of any man who can perform the feat. On the way thither, Rama brings to life Ahalya, a woman who in a former age had been changed to stone for unfaithfulness to her austere husband, and had been condemned to remain a stone until trodden by Rama's foot. Without further adventure, they reach Mithila, where the hermit presents Rama as a candidate for the bending of the bow.

The king beheld the boy, with beauty blest
  And famous lineage; he sadly thought
How hard it was to bend the bow, distressed
  Because his child must be so dearly bought.

He said: " O holy one, a mighty deed
  That full-grown elephants with greatest pain
Could hardly be successful in, we need
  Not ask of elephant-cubs. It would be vain.

For many splendid kings of valorous name,
  Bearing the scars of many a hard-fought day,
Have tried and failed; then, covered with their shame,
  Have shrugged their shoulders, cursed, and strode away."

Yet when the bow is given to the youthful Rama, he not only bends, but breaks it. He is immediately rewarded with the hand of the Princess Sita, while Lakshmana marries her sister. On their journey home with their young brides, dreadful portents appear, followed by their cause, a strange being called Rama-with-the-axe, who is carefully to be distinguished from Prince Rama. This Rama-with-the-axe is a Brahman who has sworn to exterminate the entire warrior caste, and who naturally attacks the valorous prince. He makes light of Rama's achievement in breaking Shiva's bow, and challenges him to bend the mightier bow which he carries. This the prince succeeds in doing, and Rama-with-the-axe disappears, shamed and defeated. The marriage party then continues its journey to Ayodhya.

Twelfth canto. The killing of Ravana.—King Dasharatha prepares to anoint Rama crown prince, when Queen Kaikeyi interposes. On an earlier occasion she had rendered the king a service and received his promise that he would grant her two boons, whatever she desired. She now demands her two boons: the banishment of Rama for fourteen years, and the anointing of her own son Bharata as crown prince. Rama thereupon sets out for the Dandaka forest in Southern India, accompanied by his faithful wife Sita and his devoted brother Lakshmana. The stricken father dies of grief, thus fulfilling the hermit's curse. Now Prince Bharata proves himself more generous than his mother; he refuses the kingdom, and is with great difficulty persuaded by Rama himself to act as regent during the fourteen years. Even so, he refuses to enter the capital city, dwelling in a village outside the walls, and preserving Rama's slippers as a symbol of the rightful king. Meanwhile Rama's little party penetrates the wild forests of the south, fighting as need arises with the giants there. Unfortunately, a giantess falls in love with Rama, and

> In Sita's very presence told
> Her birth—love made her overbold:
> For mighty passion, as a rule,
> Will change a woman to a fool.

Scorned by Rama, laughed at by Sita, she becomes furious and threatening.

> Laugh on! Your laughter's fruit shall be
> Commended to you. Gaze on me!
> I am a tigress, you shall know,
> Insulted by a feeble doe.

Lakshmana thereupon cuts off her nose and ears, rendering her redundantly hideous. She departs, to return presently at the head of an army of giants, whom Rama defeats single-handed, while his brother guards Sita. The giantess then betakes herself to her brother, the terrible ten-headed Ravana, king of Ceylon. He succeeds in capturing Sita by a trick, and carries her off to his fortress in Ceylon. It is plainly necessary for Rama to seek allies before attempting to cross the straits and attack the stronghold. He therefore renders an important service to the monkey king Sugriva, who gratefully leads an army of monkeys to his assistance. The most valiant of these, Hanumat, succeeds in entering Ravana's capital, where he finds Sita, gives her a token from Rama, and receives a token for Rama. The army thereupon sets out and comes to the seashore, where it is reinforced by the giant Vibhishana, who has deserted his wicked brother Ravana. The monkeys hurl great boulders into the strait, thus forming a bridge over which they cross into Ceylon and besiege Ravana's capital. There ensue many battles between the giants and the monkeys, culminating in a tremendous duel between the champions, Rama and Ravana. In this duel Ravana is finally slain. Rama recovers his wife, and the principal personages of the army enter the flying chariot which had belonged to Ravana, to return to Ayodhya; for the fourteen years of exile are now over.

Thirteenth canto. The return from the forest.—This canto describes the long journey through the air from Ceylon over the whole length of India to Ayodhya. As the celestial car makes its journey, Rama points out the objects of interest or of memory to Sita. Thus, as they fly over the sea:

> The form of ocean, infinitely changing,
> Clasping the world and all its gorgeous state,

Unfathomed by the intellect's wide ranging,
  Is awful like the form of God, and great.

He gives his billowy lips to many a river
  That into his embrace with passion slips,
Lover of many wives, a generous giver
  Of kisses, yet demanding eager lips.

Look back, my darling, with your fawn-like glances
  Upon the path that from your prison leads;
See how the sight of land again entrances,
  How fair the forest, as the sea recedes.

Then, as they pass over the spot where Rama searched for his stolen wife:

There is the spot where, sorrowfully searching,
  I found an anklet on the ground one day;
It could not tinkle, for it was not perching
  On your dear foot, but sad and silent lay.

I learned where you were carried by the giant
  From vines that showed themselves compassionate;
They could not utter words, yet with their pliant
  Branches they pointed where you passed of late.

The deer were kind; for while the juicy grasses
  Fell quite unheeded from each careless mouth,
They turned wide eyes that said, " 'Tis there she passes
  The hours as weary captive " toward the south.

There is the mountain where the peacocks' screaming,
  And branches smitten fragrant by the rain,
And madder-flowers that woke at last from dreaming,
  Made unendurable my lonely pain;

And mountain-caves where I could scarce dissemble
  The woe I felt when thunder crashed anew,
For I remembered how you used to tremble
  At thunder, seeking arms that longed for you.

Rama then points out the spots in Southern India where he and Sita had dwelt in exile, and the pious hermitages which they had visited; later, the holy spot where the Jumna River joins the Ganges; finally, their distant home, unseen for fourteen years, and the well-known river, from which spray-laden breezes come to them like cool, welcoming hands. When they draw near, Prince Bharata comes forth to welcome them, and the happy procession approaches the capital city.

Fourteenth canto. Sita is put away.—The exiles are welcomed by Queen Kausalya and Queen Sumitra with a joy tinged with deep melancholy. After the long-deferred anointing of Rama as king, comes the triumphal entry into the ancestral capital, where Rama begins his virtuous reign with his beloved queen most happily; for the very hardships endured in the forest turn into pleasures when remembered in the palace. To crown the king's joy, Sita becomes pregnant, and expresses a wish to visit the forest again. At this point, where an ordinary story would end, comes the great tragedy, the tremendous test of Rama's character. The people begin to murmur about the queen, believing that she could not have preserved her purity in the giant's palace. Rama knows that she is innocent, but he also knows that he cannot be a good king while the people feel as they do; and after a pitiful struggle, he decides to put away his beloved wife. He bids his brother Lakshmana take her to the forest, in accordance with her request, but to leave her there at the hermitage of the sage Valmiki. When this is done, and Sita hears the terrible future from Lakshmana, she cries:

Take reverent greeting to the queens, my mothers,
  And say to each with honour due her worth:
" My child is your son's child, and not another's;
  Oh, pray for him, before he comes to birth."

And tell the king from me: " You saw the matter,
  How I was guiltless proved in fire divine;
Will you desert me for mere idle chatter?
  Are such things done in Raghu's royal line?

Ah no! I cannot think you fickle-minded,
For you were always very kind to me;
Fate's thunderclap by which my eyes are blinded
Rewards my old, forgotten sins, I see.

Oh, I could curse my life and quickly end it,
For it is useless, lived from you apart,
But that I bear within, and must defend it,
Your life, your child and mine, beneath my heart.

When he is born, I'll scorn my queenly station,
Gaze on the sun, and live a hell on earth,
That I may know no pain of separation
From you, my husband, in another birth.

My king! Eternal duty bids you never
Forget a hermit who for sorrow faints;
Though I am exiled from your bed for ever,
I claim the care you owe to all the saints."

So she accepts her fate with meek courage. But

When Rama's brother left her there to languish
And bore to them she loved her final word,
She loosed her throat in an excess of anguish
And screamed as madly as a frightened bird.

Trees shed their flowers, the peacock-dances ended,
The grasses dropped from mouths of feeding deer,
As if the universal forest blended
Its tears with hers, and shared her woeful fear.

While she laments thus piteously, she is discovered by the poet-sage Valmiki, who consoles her with tender and beautiful words, and conducts her to his hermitage, where she awaits the time of her confinement. Meanwhile Rama leads a dreary life, finding duty but a cold comforter. He makes a golden statue of his wife, and will not look at other women.

Fifteenth canto. Rama goes to heaven.—The canto opens with a rather long description of a fight between Rama's youngest brother and a giant. On the journey to meet the giant, Shatrughna spends a night in Valmiki's hermitage, and that very night Sita gives birth to twin sons. Valmiki gives them the names Kusha and Lava, and when they grow out of childhood he teaches them his own composition, the *Ramayana*, " the sweet story of Rama," " the first path shown to poets." At this time the young son of a Brahman dies in the capital, and the father laments at the king's gate, for he believes that the king is unworthy, else heaven would not send death prematurely. Rama is roused to stamp out evil-doing in the kingdom, whereupon the dead boy comes to life. The king then feels that his task on earth is nearly done, and prepares to celebrate the great horse-sacrifice.[1] At this sacrifice appear the two youths Kusha and Lava, who sing the epic of Rama's deeds in the presence of Rama himself. The father perceives their likeness to himself, then learns that they are indeed his children, whom he has never seen. Thereupon Sita is brought forward by the poet-sage Valmiki and in the presence of her husband and her detractors establishes her constant purity in a terrible fashion.

" If I am faithful to my lord
In thought, in action, and in word,
I pray that Earth who bears us all
May bid me in her bosom fall."

The faithful wife no sooner spoke
Than earth divided, and there broke
From deep within a flashing light
That flamed like lightning, blinding-bright.

And, seated on a splendid throne
Upheld by serpents' hoods alone,
The goddess Earth rose visibly,
And she was girded with the sea.

Sita was clasped in her embrace,
While still she gazed on Rama's face:
He cried aloud in wild despair;
She sank, and left him standing there.

Rama then establishes his brothers, sons, and nephews in

[1] See footnote, p. 128.

different cities of the kingdom, buries the three queens of his father, and awaits death. He has not long to wait; Death comes, wearing a hermit's garb, asks for a private interview, and threatens any who shall disturb their conference. Lakshmana disturbs them, and so dies before Rama. Then Rama is translated.

Cantos sixteen to nineteen form the third division of the epic, and treat of Rama's descendants. The interest wanes, for the great hero is gone.

Sixteenth canto. Kumudvati's wedding.—As Kusha lies awake one night, a female figure appears in his chamber; and in answer to his question, declares that she is the presiding goddess of the ancient capital Ayodhya, which has been deserted since Rama's departure to heaven. She pictures the sad state of the city thus:

I have no king; my towers and terraces
  Crumble and fall; my walls are overthrown;
As when the ugly winds of evening seize
  The rack of clouds in helpless darkness blown.

In streets where maidens gaily passed at night,
  Where once was known the tinkle and the shine
Of anklets, jackals slink, and by the light
  Of flashing fangs, seek carrion, snarl, and whine.

The water of the pools that used to splash
  With drumlike music, under maidens' hands,
Groans now when bisons from the jungle lash
  It with their clumsy horns, and roil its sands.

The peacock-pets are wild that once were tame;
  They roost on trees, not perches; lose desire
For dancing to the drums; and feel no shame
  For fans singed close by sparks of forest-fire.

On stairways where the women once were glad
  To leave their pink and graceful footprints, here
Unwelcome, blood-stained paws of tigers pad,
  Fresh-smeared from slaughter of the forest deer.

Wall-painted elephants in lotus-brooks,
  Receiving each a lily from his mate,
Are torn and gashed, as if by cruel hooks,
  By claws of lions, showing furious hate.

I see my pillared caryatides
  Neglected, weathered, stained by passing time,
Wearing in place of garments that should please,
  The skins of sloughing cobras, foul with slime.

The balconies grow black with long neglect,
  And grass-blades sprout through floors no longer tight;
They still receive but cannot now reflect
  The old, familiar moonbeams, pearly white.

The vines that blossomed in my garden bowers,
  That used to show their graceful beauty, when
Girls gently bent their twigs and plucked their flowers,
  Are broken by wild apes and wilder men.

The windows are not lit by lamps at night,
  Nor by fair faces shining in the day,
But webs of spiders dim the delicate, light
  Smoke-tracery with one mere daub of grey.

The river is deserted; on the shore
  No gaily bathing men and maidens leave
Food for the swans; its reedy bowers no more
  Are vocal: seeing this, I can but grieve.

The goddess therefore begs Kusha to return with his court to the old capital, and when he assents, she smiles and vanishes. The next morning Kusha announces the vision of the night, and immediately sets out for Ayodhya with his whole army. Arrived there, King Kusha quickly restores the city to its former splendour. Then when the hot summer comes, the king goes down to the river to bathe with the ladies of the court. While in the water he loses a great gem which his father had given him. The divers are unable to find it, and declare their belief that it has been stolen by the serpent Kumuda who lives in the river. The king threatens to shoot an arrow into the river, whereupon the waters divide, and the serpent appears with the gem. He is accompanied by a beautiful maiden, whom he introduces as his sister Kumudvati, and whom he offers in marriage to Kusha. The offer is accepted, and the wedding celebrated with great pomp.

Seventeenth canto. King Atithi.—To the king and queen is born a son, who is named Atithi. When he has grown into manhood, his father Kusha engages in a struggle with a demon, in which the king is killed in the act of killing his adversary. He goes to heaven, followed by his faithful queen, and Atithi is anointed king. The remainder of the canto describes King Atithi's glorious reign.

Eighteenth canto. The later princes.—This canto gives a brief, impressionistic sketch of the twenty-one kings who in their order succeeded Atithi.

Nineteenth canto. The loves of Agnivarna.—After the twenty-one kings just mentioned, there succeeds a king named Agnivarna, who gives himself to dissipation. He shuts himself up in the palace; even when duty requires him to appear before his subjects, he does so merely by hanging one foot out of a window. He trains dancing-girls himself, and has so many mistresses that he cannot always call them by their right names. It is not wonderful that this kind of life leads before long to a consuming disease; and as Agnivarna is even then unable to resist the pleasures of the senses, he dies. His queen is pregnant, and she mounts the throne as regent in behalf of her unborn son. With this strange scene, half tragic, half vulgar, the epic, in the form in which it has come down to us, abruptly ends.

If we now endeavour to form some critical estimate of the poem, we are met at the outset by this strangely unnatural termination. We cannot avoid wondering whether the poem as we have it is complete. And we shall find that there are good reasons for believing that Kalidasa did not let the glorious solar line end in the person of the voluptuous Agnivarna and his unborn child. In the first place, there is a constant tradition which affirms that *The Dynasty of Raghu* originally consisted of twenty-five cantos. A similar tradition concerning Kalidasa's second epic has justified itself; for some time only seven cantos were known; then more were discovered, and we now have seventeen. Again, there is a rhetorical rule, almost never disregarded, which requires a literary work to end with an epilogue in the form of a little prayer for the welfare of readers or auditors. Kalidasa himself complies with this rule, certainly in five of his other six books. Once again, Kalidasa has nothing of the tragedian in his soul; his works, without exception, end happily. In the drama *Urvashi* he seriously injures a splendid old tragic story for the sake of a happy ending. These facts all point to the probability that the conclusion of the epic has been lost. We may even assign a natural, though conjectural, reason for this. *The Dynasty of Raghu* has been used for centuries as a text-book in India, so that manuscripts abound, and commentaries are very numerous. Now if the concluding cantos were unfitted for use as a text-book, they might very easily be lost during the centuries before the introduction of printing-presses into India. Indeed, this very unfitness for use as a school text seems to be the explanation of the temporary loss of several cantos of Kalidasa's second epic.

On the other hand, we are met by the fact that numerous commentators, living in different parts of India, know the text of only nineteen cantos. Furthermore, it is unlikely that Kalidasa left the poem incomplete at his death; for it was, without serious question, one of his earlier works. Apart from evidences of style, there is the subject-matter of the introductory stanzas, in which the poet presents himself as an aspirant for literary fame. No writer of established reputation would be likely to say:

> The fool who seeks a poet's fame,
> Must look for ridicule and blame,
> Like tiptoe dwarf who fain would try
> To pluck the fruit for giants high.

In only one other of his writings, in the drama which was undoubtedly written earlier than the other two dramas, does the poet thus present his feeling of diffidence to his auditors.

It is of course possible that Kalidasa wrote the first nineteen cantos when a young man, intending to add more, then turned to other matters, and never afterwards cared to take up the rather thankless task of ending a youthful work.

The question does not admit of final solution. Yet whoever reads and re-reads *The Dynasty of Raghu,* and the other works of its author, finds the conviction growing ever stronger that our poem in nineteen cantos is mutilated. We are thus enabled to clear the author of the charge of a lame and impotent conclusion.

Another adverse criticism cannot so readily be disposed of; that of a lack of unity in the plot. As the poem treats of a kingly dynasty, we frequently meet the cry: The king is dead. Long live the king! The story of Rama himself occupies only six cantos; he is not born until the tenth canto, he is in heaven after the fifteenth. There are in truth six heroes, each of whom has to die to make room for his successor. One may go farther and say that it is not possible to give a brief and accurate title to the poem. It is not a *Ramayana,* or epic of Rama's deeds, for Rama is on the stage during only a third of the poem. It is not properly an epic of Raghu's line, for many kings of this line are unmentioned. Not merely kings who escape notice by their obscurity, but also several who fill a large place in Indian story, whose deeds and adventures are splendidly worthy of epic treatment. *The Dynasty of Raghu* is rather an epic poem in which Rama is the central figure, giving it such unity as it possesses, but which provides Rama with a most generous background in the shape of selected episodes concerning his ancestors and his descendants.

Rama is the central figure. Take him away and the poem falls to pieces like a pearl necklace with a broken string. Yet it may well be doubted whether the cantos dealing with Rama are the most successful. They are too compressed, too briefly allusive. Kalidasa attempts to tell the story in about one-thirtieth of the space given to it by his great predecessor Valmiki. The result is much loss by omission and much loss by compression. Many of the best episodes of the *Ramayana* are quite omitted by Kalidasa: for example, the story of the jealous humpback who eggs on Queen Kaikeyi to demand her two boons; the beautiful scene in which Sita insists on following Rama into the forest; the account of the somnolent giant Pot-ear, a character quite as good as Polyphemus. Other fine episodes are so briefly alluded to as to lose all their charm: for example, the story of the golden deer that attracts the attention of Rama while Ravana is stealing his wife; the journey of the monkey Hanumat to Ravana's fortress and his interview with Sita.

The Rama-story, as told by Valmiki, is one of the great epic stories of the world. It has been for two thousand years and more the story *par excellence* of the Hindus; and the Hindus may fairly claim to be the best story-tellers of the world. There is therefore real matter for regret in the fact that so great a poet as Kalidasa should have treated it in a way not quite worthy of it and of himself. The reason is not far to seek, nor can there be any reasonable doubt as to its truth. Kalidasa did not care to put himself into direct competition with Valmiki. The younger poet's admiration of his mighty predecessor is clearly expressed. It is with especial reference to Valmiki that he says in his introduction:

> Yet I may enter through the door
> That mightier poets pierced of yore;
> A thread may pierce a jewel, but
> Must follow where the diamond cut.

He introduces Valmiki into his own epic, making him compose the *Ramayana* in Rama's lifetime. Kalidasa speaks of Valmiki as "the poet," and the great epic he calls "the sweet story of Rama," "the first path shown to poets," which, when sung by the two boys, was heard with motionless delight by the deer, and, when sung before a gathering of learned men, made them heedless of the tears that rolled down their cheeks.

Bearing these matters in mind, we can see the course of Kalidasa's thoughts almost as clearly as if he had expressed them directly. He was irresistibly driven to write the wonderful story of Rama, as any poet would be who became familiar with it. At the same time, his modesty prevented him from challenging the old epic directly. He therefore writes a poem which shall appeal to the hallowed associations that cluster round the great name of Rama, but devotes two-thirds of it to themes that permit him greater freedom. The result is a formless plot.

This is a real weakness, yet not a fatal weakness. In general, literary critics lay far too much emphasis on plot. Of the elements that make a great book, two, style and presentation of character, hardly permit critical analysis. The third, plot, does permit such analysis. Therefore the analyst overrates its importance. It is fatal to all claim of greatness in a narrative if it is shown to have a bad style or to be without interesting characters. It is not fatal if it is shown that the plot is rambling. In recent literature it is easy to find truly great narratives in which the plot leaves much to be desired. We may cite the *Pickwick Papers, Les Misérables, War and Peace.*

We must then regard *The Dynasty of Raghu* as a poem in which single episodes take a stronger hold upon the reader than does the unfolding of an ingenious plot. In some degree, this is true of all long poems. The *Æneid* itself, the most perfect long poem ever written, has dull passages. And when this allowance is made, what wonderful passages we have in Kalidasa's poem! One hardly knows which of them makes the strongest appeal, so many are they and so varied. There is the description of the small boy Raghu in the third canto, the choice of the princess in the sixth, the lament of King Aja in the eighth, the story of Dasharatha and the hermit youth in the ninth, the account of the ruined city in the sixteenth. Besides these, the Rama cantos, ten to fifteen, make an epic within an epic. And if Kalidasa is not seen at his very best here, yet his second best is of a higher quality than the best of others. Also, the Rama story is so moving that a mere allusion to it stirs like a sentimental memory of childhood. It has the usual qualities of a good epic story: abundance of travel and fighting and adventure and magic interweaving of human with superhuman, but it has more than this. In both hero and heroine there is real development of character. Odysseus and Æneas do not grow; they go through adventures. But King Rama, torn between love for his wife and duty to his subjects, is almost a different person from the handsome, light-hearted prince who won his bride by breaking Shiva's bow. Sita, faithful to the husband who rejects her, has made a long, character-forming journey since the day when she left her father's palace, a youthful bride. Herein lies the unique beauty of the tale of Rama, that it unites romantic love and moral conflict with a splendid story of wild adventure. No wonder that the Hindus, connoisseurs of story-telling, have loved the tale of Rama's deeds better than any other story.

If we compare *The Dynasty of Raghu* with Kalidasa's other books, we find it inferior to *The Birth of the War-god* in unity of plot, inferior to *Shakuntala* in sustained interest, inferior to *The Cloud-Messenger* in perfection of every detail. Yet passages in it are as high and sweet as anything in these works. And over it is shed the magic charm of Kalidasa's style. Of that it is vain to speak. It can be had only at first hand. The final proof that *The Dynasty of Raghu* is a very great poem, is this: no one who once reads it can leave it alone thereafter.

THE BIRTH OF THE WAR-GOD

THE BIRTH OF THE WAR-GOD

The Birth of the War-god is an epic poem in seventeen cantos. It consists of 1096 stanzas, or about 4400 lines of verse. The subject is the marriage of the god Shiva, the birth of his son, and the victory of this son over a powerful demon. The story was not invented by Kalidasa, but taken from old mythology. Yet it had never been told in so masterly a fashion as had been the story of Rama's deeds by Valmiki. Kalidasa is therefore under less constraint in writing this epic than in writing *The Dynasty of Raghu.* I give first a somewhat detailed analysis of the matter of the poem.

First canto. The birth of Parvati.—The poem begins with a description of the great Himalaya mountain-range.

God of the distant north, the Snowy Range
    O'er other mountains towers imperially;
Earth's measuring-rod, being great and free from change,
    Sinks to the eastern and the western sea.

Whose countless wealth of natural gems is not
    Too deeply blemished by the cruel snow;
One fault for many virtues is forgot,
    The moon's one stain for beams that endless flow.

Where demigods enjoy the shade of clouds
    Girding his lower crests, but often seek,
When startled by the sudden rain that shrouds
    His waist, some loftier, ever sunlit peak.

Where bark of birch-trees makes, when torn in strips
    And streaked with mountain minerals that blend
To written words 'neath dainty finger-tips,
    Such dear love-letters as the fairies send.

Whose organ-pipes are stems of bamboo, which
  Are filled from cavern-winds that know no rest,
As if the mountain strove to set the pitch
  For songs that angels sing upon his crest.

Where magic herbs that glitter in the night
  Are lamps that need no oil within them, when
They fill cave-dwellings with their shimmering light
  And shine upon the loves of mountain men.

Who offers roof and refuge in his caves
  To timid darkness shrinking from the day;
A lofty soul is generous; he saves
  Such honest cowards as for protection pray.

Who brings to birth the plants of sacrifice;
  Who steadies earth, so strong is he and broad.
The great Creator, for this service' price,
  Made him the king of mountains, and a god.

Himalaya marries a wife, to whom in course of time a daughter is born, as wealth is born when ambition pairs with character. The child is named Parvati, that is, daughter of the mountain. Her father takes infinite delight in her, as well he may; for

She brought him purity and beauty too,
  As white flames to the lamp that burns at night;
Or Ganges to the path whereby the true
  Reach heaven; or judgment to the erudite.

She passes through a happy childhood of sand-piles, balls, dolls, and little girl friends, when all at once young womanhood comes upon her.

As pictures waken to the painter's brush,
  Or lilies open to the morning sun,
Her perfect beauty answered to the flush
  Of womanhood when childish days were done.

Suppose a blossom on a leafy spray;
  Suppose a pearl on spotless coral laid:
Such was the smile, pure, radiantly gay,
  That round her red, red lips for ever played.

And when she spoke, the music of her tale
  Was sweet, the music of her voice to suit,
Till listeners felt as if the nightingale
  Had grown discordant like a jangled lute.

It is predicted by a heavenly being that she will one day become the wife of the god Shiva. This prediction awakens her father's pride, and also his impatience, since Shiva makes no advances. For the destined bridegroom is at this time leading a life of stern austerity and self-denial upon a mountain peak. Himalaya therefore bids his daughter wait upon Shiva. She does so, but without being able to divert him from his austerities.

Second canto. Brahma's self-revelation.—At this time, the gods betake themselves to Brahma, the Creator, and sing a hymn of praise, a part of which is given here.

Before creation, thou art one;
Three, when creation's work is done:
All praise and honour unto thee
In this thy mystic trinity.

Three various forms and functions three
Proclaim thy living majesty;
Thou dost create, and then maintain,
And last, destroyest all again.

Thy slow recurrent day and night
Bring death to all, or living light.
We live beneath thy waking eye;
Thou sleepest, and thy creatures die.

Solid and fluid, great and small,
And light and heavy—Thou art all;
Matter and form are both in thee:
Thy powers are past discovery.

Thou art the objects that unroll
Their drama for the passive soul;
Thou art the soul that views the play
Indifferently, day by day.

Thou art the knower and the known;
Eater and food art thou alone;
The priest and his oblation fair;
The prayerful suppliant and the prayer.

Brahma receives their worship graciously, and asks the reason of their coming. The spokesman of the gods explains to Brahma how a great demon named Taraka is troubling the world, and how helpless they are in opposing him. They have tried the most extravagant propitiation, and found it useless.

The sun in heaven dare not glow
With undiminished heat, but so
As that the lilies may awake
Which blossom in his pleasure-lake.

The wind blows gently as it can
To serve him as a soothing fan,
And dare not manifest its power,
Lest it should steal a garden flower.

The seasons have forgotten how
To follow one another now;
They simultaneously bring
Him flowers of autumn, summer, spring.

Such adoration makes him worse;
He troubles all the universe:
Kindness inflames a rascal's mind;
He should be recompensed in kind.

And all the means that we have tried
Against the rogue, are brushed aside,
As potent herbs have no avail
When bodily powers begin to fail.

We seek a leader, O our Lord,
To bring him to his just reward—
As saints seek evermore to win
Virtue, to end life's woe and sin—

That he may guide the heavenly host,
And guard us to the uttermost,
And from our foe lead captive back
The victory which still we lack.

Brahma answers that the demon's power comes from him, and he does not feel at liberty to proceed against it; "for it is not fitting to cut down even a poison-tree that one's own hand has planted." But he promises that a son shall be born to Shiva and Parvati, who shall lead the gods to victory. With this answer the gods are perforce content, and their king, Indra, waits upon the god of love, to secure his necessary co-operation.

Third canto. The burning of Love.—Indra waits upon Love, who asks for his commands. Indra explains the matter, and asks Love to inflame Shiva with passion for Parvati. Love thereupon sets out, accompanied by his wife Charm and his friend Spring. When they reach the mountain where Shiva dwells, Spring shows his power. The snow disappears; the trees put forth blossoms; bees, deer, and birds waken to new life. The only living being that is not influenced by the sudden change of season is Shiva, who continues his meditation, unmoved. Love himself is discouraged, until he sees the beauty of Parvati, when he takes heart again. At this moment, Shiva chances to relax his meditation, and Parvati approaches to do him homage. Love seizes the lucky moment, and prepares to shoot his bewildering arrow at Shiva. But the great god sees him, and before the arrow is discharged, darts fire from his eye, whereby Love is consumed. Charm falls in a swoon, Shiva vanishes, and the wretched Parvati is carried away by her father.

Fourth canto. The lament of Charm.—This canto is given entire.

The wife of Love lay helpless in a swoon,
  Till wakened by a fate whose deadliest sting
Was preparation of herself full soon
  To taste the youthful widow's sorrowing.

Her opening eyes were fixed with anxious thought
  On every spot where he might be, in vain,
Were gladdened nowhere by the sight she sought,
  The lover she should never see again.

She rose and cried aloud: "Dost thou yet live,
  Lord of my life?" And at the last she found
Him whom the wrathful god could not forgive,
  Her Love, a trace of ashes on the ground.

With breaking heart, with lovely bosom stained
  By cold embrace of earth, with flying hair,
She wept and to the forest world complained,
  As if the forest in her grief might share.

"Thy beauty slew the pride that maidens cherish;
  Perfect its loveliness in every part;
I saw that beauty fade away and perish,
  Yet did not die. How hard is woman's heart!

Where art thou gone? Thy love a moment only
  Endured, and I for ever need its power;
Gone like the stream that leaves the lily lonely,
  When the dam breaks, to mourn her dying flower.

Thou never didst a thing to cause me anguish;
  I never did a thing to work thee harm;
Why should I thus in vain affliction languish?
  Why not return to bless thy grieving Charm?

Of playful chastisements art thou reminded,
  Thy flirtings punished by my girdle-strands,
Thine eyes by flying dust of blossoms blinded,
  Held for thy meet correction in these hands?

I loved to hear the name thou gav'st me often
  'Heart of my heart.' Alas! It was not true,
But lulling phrase, my coming grief to soften:
  Else in thy death, my life had ended, too.

Think not that on the journey thou hast taken
  So newly, I should fail to find thy track;
Ah, but the world! The world is quite forsaken,
  For life is love; no life, when thee they lack.

Thou gone, my love, what power can guide the maiden
  Through veils of midnight darkness in the town
To the eager heart with loving fancies laden,
  And fortify against the storm-cloud's frown?

The wine that teaches eyes their gladdest dances,
  That bids the love-word trippingly to glide,
Is now deception; for if flashing glances
  Lead not to love, they lead to naught beside.

And when he knows thy life is a remembrance,
  Thy friend the moon will feel his shining vain,
Will cease to show the world a circle's semblance,
  And even in his waxing time, will wane.

Slowly the mango-blossoms are unfolding
  On twigs where pink is struggling with the green,
Greeted by koïl-birds sweet concert holding—
  Thou dead, who makes of flowers an arrow keen?

Or weaves a string of bees with deft invention,
  To speed the missile when the bow is bent?
They buzz about me now with kind intention,
  And mortify the grief which they lament.

Arise! Assume again thy radiant beauty!
  Rebuke the koïl-bird, whom nature taught
Such sweet persuasion; she forgets her duty
  As messenger to bosoms passion-fraught.

Well I remember, Love, thy suppliant motion,
  Thy trembling, quick embrace, the moments blest
By fervent, self-surrendering devotion—
  And memories like these deny me rest.

Well didst thou know thy wife; the springtime garland,
  Wrought by thy hands, O charmer of thy Charm!
Remains to bid me grieve, while in a far land
  Thy body seeks repose from earthly harm.

Thy service by the cruel gods demanded,
  Meant service to thy wife left incomplete,
My bare feet with coquettish streakings banded—
  Return to end the adorning of my feet.

No, straight to thee I fly, my body given,
  A headlong moth, to quick-consuming fire,
Or e'er my cunning rivals, nymphs in heaven,
  Awake in thee an answering desire.

Yet, dearest, even this short delay is fated
  For evermore a deep reproach to prove,
A stain that may not be obliterated,
  If Charm has lived one moment far from Love.

And how can I perform the last adorning
  Of thy poor body, as befits a wife?
So strangely on the path that leaves me mourning
  Thy body followed still the spirit's life.

I see thee straighten out thy blossom-arrow,
  The bow slung careless on thy breast the while,
Thine eyes in mirthful, sidelong glance grow narrow,
  Thy conference with friendly Spring, thy smile.

But where is Spring? Dear friend, whose art could fashion
  The flowery arrow for thee? Has the wrath
Of dreadful Shiva, in excess of passion,
  Bade him, too, follow on that fatal path?"

Heart-smitten by the accents of her grief
  Like poisoned darts, soothing her fond alarm,
Incarnate Spring appeared, to bring relief
  As friendship can, to sore-lamenting Charm.

And at the sight of him, she wept the more,
  And often clutched her throat, and beat her breast;
For lamentation finds an open door
  In the presence of the friends we love the best.

Stifling, she cried: "Behold the mournful matter!
  In place of him thou seekest, what is found?
A something that the winds of heaven scatter,
  A trace of dove-grey ashes on the ground.

Arise, O Love! For Spring knows no estranging,
  Thy friend in lucky hap and evil lot;
Man's love for wife is ever doubtful, changing;
  Man's love for man abides and changes not.

With such a friend, thy dart, on dainty pinion
  Of blossoms, shot from lotus-fibre string,
Reduced men, giants, gods to thy dominion—
  The triple world has felt that arrow sting.

But Love is gone, far gone beyond returning,
  A candle snuffed by wandering breezes vain;
And see! I am his wick, with Love once burning,
  Now blackened by the smoke of nameless pain.

In slaying Love, fate wrought but half a slaughter,
  For I am left. And yet the clinging vine
Must fall, when falls the sturdy tree that taught her
  Round him in loving tenderness to twine.

So then, fulfil for me the final mission
  Of him who undertakes a kinsman's part;
Commit me to the flames (my last petition)
  And speed the widow to her husband's heart.

The moonlight wanders not, the moon forsaking;
  Where sails the cloud, the lightning is not far;
Wife follows mate, is law of nature's making,
  Yes, even among such things as lifeless are.

My breast is stained; I lay among the ashes
  Of him I loved with all a woman's powers;
Now let me lie where death-fire flames and flashes,
  As glad as on a bed of budding flowers.

Sweet Spring, thou camest oft where we lay sleeping
  On blossoms, I and he whose life is sped;
Unto the end thy friendly office keeping,
  Prepare for me the last, the fiery bed.

And fan the flame to which I am committed
  With southern winds; I would no longer stay;
Thou knowest well how slow the moments flitted
  For Love, my love, when I was far away.

And sprinkle some few drops of water, given
  In friendship, on his ashes and on me;
That Love and I may quench our thirst in heaven
  As once on earth, in heavenly unity.

And sometimes seek the grave where Love is lying;
  Pause there a moment, gentle Spring, and shower
Sweet mango-clusters to the winds replying;
  For he thou lovedst, loved the mango-flower."

As Charm prepared to end her mortal pain
  In fire, she heard a voice from heaven cry,
That showed her mercy, as the early rain
  Shows mercy to the fish, when lakes go dry:

" O wife of Love! Thy lover is not lost
  For evermore. This voice shall tell thee why
He perished like the moth, when he had crossed
  The dreadful god, in fire from Shiva's eye.

When darts of Love set Brahma in a flame,
  To shame his daughter with impure desire,
He checked the horrid sin without a name,
  And cursed the god of love to die by fire.

But Virtue interceded in behalf
  Of Love, and won a softening of the doom:
'Upon the day when Shiva's heart shall laugh
  In wedding joy, for mercy finding room,

He shall unite Love's body with the soul,
  A marriage-present to his mountain bride.'
As clouds hold fire and water in control,
  Gods are the fount of wrath, and grace beside.

So, gentle Charm, preserve thy body sweet
  For dear reunion after present pain;
The stream that dwindles in the summer heat,
  Is reunited with the autumn rain."

Invisibly and thus mysteriously
  The thoughts of Charm were turned away from death;
And Spring, believing where he might not see,
  Comforted her with words of sweetest breath.

The wife of Love awaited thus the day,
  Though racked by grief, when fate should show its power,
As the waning moon laments her darkened ray
  And waits impatient for the twilight hour.

Fifth canto. The reward of self-denial.—Parvati reproaches her own beauty, for "loveliness is fruitless if it does not bind a lover." She therefore resolves to lead a life of religious self-denial, hoping that the merit thus acquired will procure her Shiva's love. Her mother tries in vain to dissuade her; her father directs her to a fit mountain peak, and she retires to her devotions. She lays aside all ornaments, lets her hair hang unkempt, and assumes the hermit's dress of bark. While she is spending her days in self-denial, she is visited by a Brahman youth, who compliments her highly upon her rigid devotion, and declares that her conduct proves the truth of the proverb: Beauty can do no wrong. Yet he confesses himself bewildered, for she seems to have everything that heart can desire. He therefore asks her purpose in performing these austerities, and is told how her desires are fixed upon the highest of all objects, upon the god Shiva himself, and how, since Love is dead, she sees no way to win him except by ascetic religion. The youth tries to dissuade Parvati by recounting all the dreadful legends that are current about Shiva: how he wears a coiling snake on his wrist, a bloody elephant-hide upon his back, how he dwells in a graveyard, how he rides upon an undignified bull, how poor he is and of unknown birth. Parvati's anger is awakened by this recital. She frowns and her lip quivers as she defends herself and the object of her love.

Shiva, she said, is far beyond the thought
  Of such as you: then speak no more to me.
Dull crawlers hate the splendid wonders wrought
  By lofty souls untouched by rivalry.

They search for wealth, whom dreaded evil nears,
  Or they who fain would rise a little higher;
The world's sole refuge neither hopes nor fears
  Nor seeks the objects of a small desire.

Yes, he is poor, yet he is riches' source;
  This graveyard-haunter rules the world alone;
Dreadful is he, yet all beneficent force:
  Think you his inmost nature can be known?

All forms are his; and he may take or leave
  At will, the snake, or gem with lustre white;
The bloody skin, or silk of softest weave;
  Dead skulls, or moonbeams radiantly bright.

For poverty he rides upon a bull,
  While Indra, king of heaven, elephant-borne,
Bows low to strew his feet with beautiful,
  Unfading blossoms in his chaplet worn.

Yet in the slander spoken in pure hate
  One thing you uttered worthy of his worth:

How could the author of the uncreate
  Be born? How could we understand his birth?

Enough of this! Though every word that you
  Have said, be faithful, yet would Shiva please
My eager heart all made of passion true
  For him alone. Love sees no blemishes.

In response to this eloquence, the youth throws off his disguise, appearing as the god Shiva himself, and declares his love for her. Parvati immediately discontinues her religious asceticism; for "successful effort regenerates."

Sixth canto. Parvati is given in marriage.—While Parvati departs to inform her father of what has happened, Shiva summons the seven sages, who are to make the formal proposal of marriage to the bride's parents. The seven sages appear, flying through the air, and with them Arundhati, the heavenly model of wifely faith and devotion. On seeing her, Shiva feels his eagerness for marriage increase, realising that

All actions of a holy life
Are rooted in a virtuous wife.

Shiva then explains his purpose, and sends the seven sages to make the formal request for Parvati's hand. The seven sages fly to the brilliant city of Himalaya, where they are received by the mountain god. After a rather portentous interchange of compliments, the seven sages announce their errand, requesting Parvati's hand in behalf of Shiva. The father joyfully assents, and it is agreed that the marriage shall be celebrated after three days. These three days are spent by Shiva in impatient longing.

Seventh canto. Parvati's wedding.—The three days are spent in preparations for the wedding. So great is Parvati's unadorned beauty that the waiting-women can hardly take their eyes from her to inspect the wedding-dress. But the preparations are complete at last; and the bride is beautiful indeed.

As when the flowers are budding on a vine,
  Or white swans rest upon a river's shore,
Or when at night the stars in heaven shine,
  Her lovely beauty grew with gems she wore.

When wide-eyed glances gave her back the same
  Bright beauty—and the mirror never lies—
She waited with impatience till he came:
  For women dress to please their lovers' eyes.

Meanwhile Shiva finishes his preparations, and sets out on his wedding journey, accompanied by Brahma, Vishnu, and lesser gods. At his journey's end, he is received by his bride's father, and led through streets ankle-deep in flowers, where the windows are filled with the faces of eager and excited women, who gossip together thus:

For his sake it was well that Parvati
  Should mortify her body delicate;
Thrice happy might his serving-woman be,
  And infinitely blest his bosom's mate.

Shiva and his retinue then enter the palace, where he is received with bashful love by Parvati, and the wedding is celebrated with due pomp. The nymphs of heaven entertain the company with a play, and Shiva restores the body of Love.

Eighth canto. The honeymoon.—The first month of marital bliss is spent in Himalaya's palace. After this the happy pair wander for a time among the famous mountain-peaks. One of these they reach at sunset, and Shiva describes the evening glow to his bride. A few stanzas are given here.

See, my belovèd, how the sun
  With beams that o'er the water shake
From western skies has now begun
  A bridge of gold across the lake.

Upon the very tree-tops sway
  The peacocks; even yet they hold

And drink the dying light of day,
  Until their fans are molten gold.

The water-lily closes, but
  With wonderful reluctancy;
As if it troubled her to shut
  Her door of welcome to the bee.

The steeds that draw the sun's bright car,
  With bended neck and falling plume
And drooping mane, are seen afar
  To bury day in ocean's gloom.

The sun is down, and heaven sleeps:
  Thus every path of glory ends;
As high as are the scalèd steeps,
  The downward way as low descends.

Shiva then retires for meditation. On his return, he finds that his bride is peevish at being left alone even for a little time, and to soothe her, he describes the night which is now advancing. A few stanzas of this description run as follows.

The twilight glow is fading far
  And stains the west with blood-red light,
As when a reeking scimitar
  Slants upward on a field of fight.

And vision fails above, below,
  Around, before us, at our back;
The womb of night envelops slow
  The world with darkness vast and black.

Mute while the world is dazed with light,
  The smiling moon begins to rise
And, being teased by eager night,
  Betrays the secrets of the skies.

Moon-fingers move the black, black hair
  Of night into its proper place,
Who shuts her eyes, the lilies fair,
  As he sets kisses on her face.

Shiva and Parvati then drink wine brought them by the guardian goddess of the grove, and in this lovely spot they dwell happily for many years.

Ninth canto. The journey to Mount Kailasa.—One day the god of fire appears as a messenger from the gods before Shiva, to remonstrate with him for not begetting the son upon whom heaven's welfare depends. Shiva deposits his seed in Fire, who departs, bent low with the burden. Shortly afterwards the gods wait upon Shiva and Parvati, who journey with them to Mount Kailasa, the splendid dwelling-place of the god of wealth. Here also Shiva and Parvati spend happy days.

Tenth canto. The birth of Kumara.—To Indra, king of the gods, Fire betakes himself, tells his story, and begs to be relieved of his burden. Indra advises him to deposit it in the Ganges. Fire therefore travels to the Ganges, leaves Shiva's seed in the river, and departs much relieved. But now it is the turn of Ganges to be distressed, until at dawn the six Pleiades come to bathe in the river. They find Shiva's seed and lay it in a nest of reeds, where it becomes a child, Kumara, the future god of war.

Eleventh canto. The birth of Kumara, continued.—Ganges suckles the beautiful infant. But there arises a dispute for the possession of the child between Fire, Ganges, and the Pleiades. At this point Shiva and Parvati arrive, and Parvati, wondering at the beauty of the infant and at the strange quarrel, asks Shiva to whom the child belongs. When Shiva tells her that Kumara is their own child, her joy is unbounded.

Because her eyes with happy tears were dim,
  'Twas but by snatches that she saw the boy;
Yet, with her blossom-hand caressing him,
  She felt a strange, an unimagined joy.

The vision of the infant made her seem
  A flower unfolding in mysterious bliss;

Or, billowy with her joyful tears, a stream;
Or pure affection, perfect in a kiss.

Shiva conducts Parvati and the boy back to Mount Kailasa, where gods and fairies welcome them with music and dancing. Here the divine child spends the days of a happy infancy, not very different from human infancy; for he learns to walk, gets dirty in the courtyard, laughs a good deal, pulls the scanty hair of an old servant, and learns to count: "One, nine, two, ten, five, seven." These evidences of healthy development cause Shiva and Parvati the most exquisite joy.

Twelfth canto. Kumara is made general.—Indra, with the other gods, waits upon Shiva, to ask that Kumara, now a youth, may be lent to them as their leader in the campaign against Taraka. The gods are graciously received by Shiva, who asks their errand. Indra prefers their request, whereupon Shiva bids his son assume command of the gods, and slay Taraka. Great is the joy of Kumara himself, of his mother Parvati, and of Indra.

Thirteenth canto. Kumara is consecrated general.—Kumara takes an affectionate farewell of his parents, and sets out with the gods. When they come to Indra's paradise, the gods are afraid to enter, lest they find their enemy there. There is an amusing scene in which each courteously invites the others to precede him, until Kumara ends their embarrassment by leading the way. Here for the first time Kumara sees with deep respect the heavenly Ganges, Indra's garden and palace, and the heavenly city. But he becomes red-eyed with anger on beholding the devastation wrought by Taraka.

He saw departed glory, saw the state
  Neglected, ruined, sad, of Indra's city,
As of a woman with a cowardly mate:
  And all his inmost heart dissolved in pity.

He saw how crystal floors were gashed and torn
  By wanton tusks of elephants, were strewed

With skins that sloughing cobras once had worn:
  And sadness overcame him as he viewed.

He saw beside the bathing-pools the bowers
  Defiled by elephants grown overbold,
Strewn with uprooted golden lotus-flowers,
  No longer bright with plumage of pure gold,

Rough with great, jewelled columns overthrown,
  Rank with invasion of the untrimmed grass:
Shame strove with sorrow at the ruin shown,
  For heaven's foe had brought these things to pass.

Amid these sorrowful surroundings the gods gather and anoint Kumara, thus consecrating him as their general.

Fourteenth canto. The march.—Kumara prepares for battle, and marshals his army. He is followed by Indra riding on an elephant, Agni on a ram, Yama on a buffalo, a giant on a ghost, Varuna on a dolphin, and many other lesser gods. When all is ready, the army sets out on its dusty march.

Fifteenth canto. The two armies clash.—The demon Taraka is informed that the hostile army is approaching, but scorns the often-conquered Indra and the boy Kumara. Nevertheless, he prepares for battle, marshals his army, and sets forth to meet the gods. But he is beset by dreadful omens of evil.

For foul birds came, a horrid flock to see,
  Above the army of the foes of heaven,
And dimmed the sun, awaiting ravenously
  The feast of demon corpses to be given.

And monstrous snakes, as black as powdered soot,
  Spitting hot poison high into the air,
Brought terror to the army underfoot,
  And crept and coiled and crawled before them there.

The sun a sickly halo round him had;
  Coiling within it frightened eyes could see

Great, writhing serpents, enviously glad
  Because the demon's death so soon should be.

And in the very circle of the sun
  Were phantom jackals, snarling to be fed;
And with impatient haste they seemed to run
  To drink the demon's blood in battle shed.

There fell, with darting flame and blinding flash
  Lighting the farthest heavens, from on high
A thunderbolt whose agonising crash
  Brought fear and shuddering from a cloudless sky.

There came a pelting rain of blazing coals
  With blood and bones of dead men mingled in;
Smoke and weird flashes horrified their souls;
  The sky was dusty grey like asses' skin.

The elephants stumbled and the horses fell,
  The footmen jostled, leaving each his post,
The ground beneath them trembled at the swell
  Of ocean, when an earthquake shook the host.

And dogs before them lifted muzzles foul
  To see the sun that lit that awful day,
And pierced the ears of listeners with a howl
  Dreadful yet pitiful, then slunk away.

Taraka's counsellors endeavour to persuade him to turn back, but he refuses; for timidity is not numbered among his faults. As he advances even worse portents appear, and finally warning voices from heaven call upon him to desist from his undertaking. The voices assure him of Kumara's prowess and inevitable victory; they advise him to make his peace while there is yet time. But Taraka's only answer is a defiance.

"You mighty gods that flit about in heaven
  And take my foeman's part, what would you say?
Have you forgot so soon the torture given
  By shafts of mine that never miss their way?

Why should I fear before a six-days child?
  Why should you prowl in heaven and gibber shrill,
Like dogs that in an autumn night run wild,
  Like deer that sneak through forests, trembling still?

The boy whom you have chosen as your chief
  In vain upon his hermit-sire shall cry;
The upright die, if taken with a thief:
  First you shall perish, then he too shall die."

And as Taraka emphasises his meaning by brandishing his great sword, the warning spirits flee, their knees knocking together. Taraka laughs horribly, then mounts his chariot, and advances against the army of the gods. On the other side the gods advance, and the two armies clash.

Sixteenth canto. The battle between gods and demons.—This canto is entirely taken up with the struggle between the two armies. A few stanzas are given here.

As pairs of champions stood forth
To test each other's fighting worth,
The bards who knew the family fame
Proclaimed aloud each mighty name.

As ruthless weapons cut their way
Through quilted armour in the fray,
White tufts of cotton flew on high
Like hoary hairs upon the sky.

Blood-dripping swords reflected bright
The sunbeams in that awful fight;
Fire-darting like the lightning-flash,
They showed how mighty heroes clash.

The archers' arrows flew so fast,
As through a hostile breast they passed,
That they were buried in the ground,
No stain of blood upon them found.

The swords that sheaths no longer clasped,
That hands of heroes firmly grasped,
Flashed out in glory through the fight,
As if they laughed in mad delight.

And many a warrior's eager lance
Shone radiant in the eerie dance,
A curling, lapping tongue of death
To lick away the soldier's breath.

Some, panting with a bloody thirst,
Fought toward the victim chosen first,
But had a reeking path to hew
Before they had him full in view.

Great elephants, their drivers gone
And pierced with arrows, struggled on,
But sank at every step in mud
Made liquid by the streams of blood.

The warriors falling in the fray,
Whose heads the sword had lopped away,
Were able still to fetch a blow
That slew the loud-exulting foe.

The footmen thrown to Paradise
By elephants of monstrous size,
Were seized upon by nymphs above,
Exchanging battle-scenes for love.

The lancer, charging at his foe,
Would pierce him through and bring him low,
And would not heed the hostile dart
That found a lodgment in his heart.

The war-horse, though unguided, stopped
The moment that his rider dropped,
And wept above the lifeless head,
Still faithful to his master dead.

Two lancers fell with mortal wound
And still they struggled on the ground;
With bristling hair, with brandished knife,
Each strove to end the other's life.

Two slew each other in the fight;
To Paradise they took their flight;
There with a nymph they fell in love,
And still they fought in heaven above.

Two souls there were that reached the sky;
From heights of heaven they could spy
Two writhing corpses on the plain,
And knew their headless forms again.

As the struggle comes to no decisive issue, Taraka seeks out the chief gods, and charges upon them.

Seventeenth canto. Taraka is slain.—Taraka engages the principal gods and defeats them with magic weapons. When they are relieved by Kumara, the demon turns to the youthful god of war, and advises him to retire from the battle.

Stripling, you are the only son
  Of Shiva and of Parvati.
Go safe and live! Why should you run
  On certain death? Why fight with me?
Withdraw! Let sire and mother blest
Clasp living son to joyful breast.

Flee, son of Shiva, flee the host
  Of Indra drowning in the sea
That soon shall close upon his boast
  In choking waves of misery.
For Indra is a ship of stone;
Withdraw, and let him sink alone.

Kumara answers with modest firmness.

The words you utter in your pride,
  O demon-prince, are only fit;

Yet I am minded to abide
The fight, and see the end of it.
The tight-strung bow and brandished sword
Decide, and not the spoken word.

And with this the duel begins. When Taraka finds his arrows parried by Kumara, he employs the magic weapon of the god of wind. When this too is parried, he uses the magic weapon of the god of fire, which Kumara neutralises with the weapon of the god of water. As they fight on, Kumara finds an opening, and slays Taraka with his lance, to the unbounded delight of the universe.

Here the poem ends, in the form in which it has come down to us. It has been sometimes thought that we have less than Kalidasa wrote, partly because of a vague tradition that there were once twenty-three cantos, partly because the customary prayer is lacking at the end. These arguments are not very cogent. Though the concluding prayer is not given in form, yet the stanzas which describe the joy of the universe fairly fill its place. And one does not see with what matter further cantos would be concerned. The action promised in the earlier part is completed in the seventeenth canto.

It has been somewhat more formidably argued that the concluding cantos are spurious, that Kalidasa wrote only the first seven or perhaps the first eight cantos. Yet, after all, what do these arguments amount to? Hardly more than this, that the first eight cantos are better poetry than the last nine. As if a poet were always at his best, even when writing on a kind of subject not calculated to call out his best. Fighting is not Kalidasa's *forte;* love is. Even so, there is great vigour in the journey of Taraka, the battle, and the duel. It may not be the highest kind of poetry, but it is wonderfully vigorous poetry of its kind. And if we reject the last nine cantos, we fall into a very much greater difficulty. The poem would be glaringly incomplete, its early promise obviously disregarded. We should have a *Birth of the War-god* in which the poet stopped before the war-god was born.

There seems then no good reason to doubt that we have the epic substantially as Kalidasa wrote it. Plainly, it has a unity which is lacking in Kalidasa's other epic, *The Dynasty of Raghu*, though in this epic, too, the interest shifts. Parvati's love-affair is the matter of the first half, Kumara's fight with the demon the matter of the second half. Further, it must be admitted that the interest runs a little thin. Even in India, where the world of gods runs insensibly into the world of men, human beings take more interest in the adventures of men than of gods. The gods, indeed, can hardly have adventures; they must be victorious. *The Birth of the War-god* pays for its greater unity by a poverty of adventure.

It would be interesting if we could know whether this epic was written before or after *The Dynasty of Raghu*. But we have no data for deciding the question, hardly any for even arguing it. The introduction to *The Dynasty of Raghu* seems, indeed, to have been written by a poet who yet had his spurs to win. But this is all.

As to the comparative excellence of the two epics, opinions differ. My own preference is for *The Dynasty of Raghu*, yet there are passages in *The Birth of the War-god* of a piercing beauty which the world can never let die.

THE CLOUD-MESSENGER

THE CLOUD-MESSENGER

In *The Cloud-Messenger* Kalidasa created a new *genre* in Sanskrit literature. Hindu critics class the poem with *The Dynasty of Raghu* and *The Birth of the War-god* as a *kavya*, or learned epic. This it obviously is not. It is fair enough to call it an elegiac poem, though a precisian might object to the term.

We have already seen, in speaking of *The Dynasty of Raghu*, what admiration Kalidasa felt for his great predecessor Valmiki, the author of the *Ramayana ;* and it is quite possible that an episode of the early epic suggested to him the idea which he has exquisitely treated in *The Cloud-Messenger*. In the *Ramayana*, after the defeat and death of Ravana, Rama returns with his wife and certain heroes of the struggle from Ceylon to his home in Northern India. The journey, made in an aërial car, gives the author an opportunity to describe the country over which the car must pass in travelling from one end of India to the other. The hint thus given him was taken by Kalidasa; a whole canto of *The Dynasty of Raghu* (the thirteenth) is concerned with the aërial journey. Now if, as seems not improbable, *The Dynasty of Raghu* was the earliest of Kalidasa's more ambitious works, it is perhaps legitimate to imagine him, as he wrote this canto, suddenly inspired with the plan of *The Cloud-Messenger*.

This plan is slight and fanciful. A demigod, in consequence of some transgression against his master, the god of wealth, is condemned to leave his home in the Himalayas, and spend a year of exile on a peak in the Vindhya Mountains, which divide the Deccan from the Ganges basin. He wishes to comfort and encourage his wife, but has no messenger to send her. In his despair, he begs a passing cloud to carry his words. He finds it necessary to describe the long journey which the cloud must take, and, as the two termini are skilfully chosen, the journey involves a visit to many of the spots famous in Indian story. The description of these spots fills the first half of the poem. The second half is filled with a more minute description of the heavenly city, of the home and bride of the demigod, and with the message proper. The proportions of the poem may appear unfortunate to the Western reader, in whom the proper names of the first half will wake scanty associations. Indeed, it is no longer possible to identify all the places mentioned, though the general route followed by the cloud can be easily traced. The peak from which he starts is probably one near the modern Nagpore. From this peak he flies a little west of north to the Nerbudda River, and the city of Ujjain; thence pretty straight north to the upper Ganges and the Himalaya. The geography of the magic city of Alaka is quite mythical.

The Cloud-Messenger contains one hundred and fifteen four-line stanzas, in a majestic metre called the "slow-stepper." The English stanza which has been chosen for the translation gives perhaps as fair a representation of the original movement as may be, where direct imitation is out of the question. Though the stanza of the translation has five lines to four for the slow-stepper, it contains fewer syllables; a constant check on the temptation to padding.

The analysis which accompanies the poem, and which is inserted in Italics at the beginning of each stanza, has more than one object. It saves footnotes; it is intended as a real help to comprehension; and it is an eminently Hindu device. Indeed, it was my first intention to translate literally portions of Mallinatha's famous commentary; and though this did not prove everywhere feasible, there is nothing in the analysis except matter suggested by the commentary.

One minor point calls for notice. The word Himálaya has been accented on the second syllable wherever it occurs. This accent is historically correct, and has some foothold in English usage; besides, it is more euphonious and better adapted to the needs of the metre.

FORMER CLOUD

I

A Yaksha, or divine attendant on Kubera, god of wealth, is exiled for a year from his home in the Himalayas. As he dwells on a peak in the Vindhya range, half India separates him from his young bride.

On Rama's shady peak where hermits roam,
Mid streams by Sita's bathing sanctified,
An erring Yaksha made his hapless home,
Doomed by his master humbly to abide,
And spend a long, long year of absence from his bride.

II

After eight months of growing emaciation, the first cloud warns him of the approach of the rainy season, when neglected brides are wont to pine and die.

Some months were gone; the lonely lover's pain
Had loosed his golden bracelet day by day
Ere he beheld the harbinger of rain,
A cloud that charged the peak in mimic fray,
As an elephant attacks a bank of earth in play.

III

Before this cause of lovers' hopes and fears
Long time Kubera's bondman sadly bowed
In meditation, choking down his tears—
Even happy hearts thrill strangely to the cloud;
To him, poor wretch, the loved embrace was disallowed.

IV

Unable to send tidings otherwise of his health and unchanging love, he resolves to make the cloud his messenger.

Longing to save his darling's life, unblest
With joyous tidings, through the rainy days,
He plucked fresh blossoms for his cloudy guest,
Such homage as a welcoming comrade pays,
And bravely spoke brave words of greeting and of praise.

V

Nor did it pass the lovelorn Yaksha's mind
How all unfitly might his message mate
With a cloud, mere fire and water, smoke and wind—
Ne'er yet was lover could discriminate
'Twixt life and lifeless things, in his love-blinded state.

VI

He prefers his request,

I know, he said, thy far-famed princely line,
Thy state, in heaven's imperial council chief,
Thy changing forms; to thee, such fate is mine,
I come a suppliant in my widowed grief—
Better thy lordly " no " than meaner souls' relief.

VII

O cloud, the parching spirit stirs thy pity;
My bride is far, through royal wrath and might;
Bring her my message to the Yaksha city,
Rich-gardened Alaka, where radiance bright
From Shiva's crescent bathes the palaces in light.

VIII

hinting at the same time that the cloud will find his kindly labour rewarded by pleasures on the road,

When thou art risen to airy paths of heaven,
Through lifted curls the wanderer's love shall peep
And bless the sight of thee for comfort given;
Who leaves his bride through cloudy days to weep
Except he be like me, whom chains of bondage keep?

IX

and by happy omens.

While favouring breezes waft thee gently forth,
And while upon thy left the plover sings
His proud, sweet song, the cranes who know thy worth
Will meet thee in the sky on joyful wings
And for delights anticipated join their rings.

X

He assures the cloud that his bride is neither dead nor faithless ;

Yet hasten, O my brother, till thou see—
Counting the days that bring the lonely smart—
The faithful wife who only lives for me:
A drooping flower is woman's loving heart,
Upheld by the stem of hope when two true lovers part.

XI

further, that there will be no lack of travelling companions.

And when they hear thy welcome thunders break,
When mushrooms sprout to greet thy fertile weeks,
The swans who long for the Himalayan lake
Will be thy comrades to Kailasa's peaks,
With juicy bits of lotus-fibre in their beaks.

XII

One last embrace upon this mount bestow
Whose flanks were pressed by Rama's holy feet,
Who yearly strives his love for thee to show,
Warmly his well-belovèd friend to greet
With the tear of welcome shed when two long-parted meet.

XIII

He then describes the long journey,

Learn first, O cloud, the road that thou must go,
Then hear my message ere thou speed away;
Before thee mountains rise and rivers flow:
When thou art weary, on the mountains stay,
And when exhausted, drink the rivers' driven spray.

XIV

beginning with the departure from Rama's peak, where dwells a company of Siddhas, divine beings of extraordinary sanctity.

Elude the heavenly elephants' clumsy spite;
Fly from this peak in richest jungle drest;
And Siddha maids who view thy northward flight
Will upward gaze in simple terror, lest
The wind be carrying quite away the mountain crest.

XV

Bright as a heap of flashing gems, there shines
Before thee on the ant-hill, Indra's bow;
Matched with that dazzling rainbow's glittering lines,
Thy sombre form shall find its beauties grow,
Like the dark herdsman Vishnu, with peacock-plumes aglow.

XVI

The Mala plateau.

The farmers' wives on Mala's lofty lea,
Though innocent of all coquettish art,
Will give thee loving glances; for on thee
Depends the fragrant furrow's fruitful part;
Thence, barely westering, with lightened burden start.

XVII

The Mango Peak.

The Mango Peak whose forest fires were laid
By streams of thine, will soothe thy weariness;
In memory of a former service paid,
Even meaner souls spurn not in time of stress
A suppliant friend; a soul so lofty, much the less.

XVIII

With ripened mango-fruits his margins teem;
And thou, like wetted braids, art blackness quite;
When resting on the mountain, thou wilt seem
Like the dark nipple on Earth's bosom white,
For mating gods and goddesses a thrilling sight.

XIX

The Reva, or Nerbudda River, foaming against the mountain side,

His bowers are sweet to forest maidens ever;
Do thou upon his crest a moment bide,
Then fly, rain-quickened, to the Reva river
Which gaily breaks on Vindhya's rocky side,
Like painted streaks upon an elephant's dingy hide.

XX

and flavoured with the ichor which exudes from the temples of elephants during the mating season.

Where thick rose-apples make the current slow,
Refresh thyself from thine exhausted state
With ichor-pungent drops that fragrant flow;
Thou shalt not then to every wind vibrate—
Empty means ever light, and full means added weight.

XXI

Spying the madder on the banks, half brown,
Half green with shoots that struggle to the birth,
Nibbling where early plantain-buds hang down,
Scenting the sweet, sweet smell of forest earth,
The deer will trace thy misty track that ends the dearth.

XXII

Though thou be pledged to ease my darling's pain,
Yet I foresee delay on every hill
Where jasmines blow, and where the peacock-train
Cries forth with joyful tears a welcome shrill;
Thy sacrifice is great, but haste thy journey still.

XXIII

The Dasharna country,

At thine approach, Dasharna land is blest
With hedgerows where gay buds are all aglow,
With village trees alive with many a nest
Abuilding by the old familiar crow,
With lingering swans, with ripe rose-apples' darker show.

XXIV

and its capital Vidisha, on the banks of Reed River.

There shalt thou see the royal city, known
Afar, and win the lover's fee complete,
If thou subdue thy thunders to a tone
Of murmurous gentleness, and taste the sweet,
Love-rippling features of the river at thy feet.

XXV

A moment rest on Nichais' mountain then,
Where madder-bushes don their blossom coat
As thrilling to thy touch; where city men
O'er youth's unbridled pleasures fondly gloat
In caverns whence the perfumes of gay women float.

XXVI

Fly on refreshed; and sprinkle buds that fade
On jasmine-vines in gardens wild and rare
By forest rivers; and with loving shade
Caress the flower-girls' heated faces fair,
Whereon the lotuses droop withering from their hair.

XXVII

The famous old city of Ujjain, the home of the poet, and dearly beloved by him ;

Swerve from thy northern path; for westward rise
The palace balconies thou mayst not slight
In fair Ujjain; and if bewitching eyes
That flutter at thy gleams, should not delight
Thine amorous bosom, useless were thy gift of sight.

XXVIII

and the river, personified as a loving woman, whom the cloud will meet just before he reaches the city.

The neighbouring mountain stream that gliding grants
A glimpse of charms in whirling eddies pursed,
While noisy swans accompany her dance
Like a tinkling zone, will slake thy loving thirst—
A woman always tells her love in gestures first.

XXIX

Thou only, happy lover! canst repair
The desolation that thine absence made:
Her shrinking current seems the careless hair
That brides deserted wear in single braid,
And dead leaves falling give her face a paler shade.

XXX

The city of Ujjain is fully described,

Oh, fine Ujjain! Gem to Avanti given,
Where village ancients tell their tales of mirth
And old romance! Oh, radiant bit of heaven,
Home of a blest celestial band whose worth
Sufficed, though fallen from heaven, to bring down heaven on earth!

XXXI

Where the river-breeze at dawn, with fragrant gain
From friendly lotus-blossoms, lengthens out
The clear, sweet passion-warbling of the crane,
To cure the women's languishing, and flout
With a lover's coaxing all their hesitating doubt.

XXXII

Enriched with odours through the windows drifting
From perfumed hair, and greeted as a friend
By peacock pets their wings in dances lifting,
On flower-sweet balconies thy labour end,
Where prints of dear pink feet an added glory lend.

XXXIII

especially its famous shrine to Shiva, called Mahakala;

Black as the neck of Shiva, very God,
Dear therefore to his hosts, thou mayest go
To his dread shrine, round which the gardens nod
When breezes rich with lotus-pollen blow
And ointments that the gaily bathing maidens know.

XXXIV

Reaching that temple at another time,
Wait till the sun is lost to human eyes;
For if thou mayest play the part sublime
Of Shiva's drum at evening sacrifice,
Then hast thou in thy thunders grave a priceless prize.

XXXV

The women there, whose girdles long have tinkled
In answer to the dance, whose hands yet seize
And wave their fans with lustrous gems besprinkled,
Will feel thine early drops that soothe and please,
And recompense thee from black eyes like clustering bees.

XXXVI

and the black cloud, painted with twilight red, is bidden to serve as a robe for the god, instead of the bloody elephant hide which he commonly wears in his wild dance.

Clothing thyself in twilight's rose-red glory,
Embrace the dancing Shiva's tree-like arm;
He will prefer thee to his mantle gory
And spare his grateful goddess-bride's alarm,
Whose eager gaze will manifest no fear of harm.

XXXVII

After one night of repose in the city,

Where women steal to rendezvous by night
Through darkness that a needle might divide,
Show them the road with lightning-flashes bright
As golden streaks upon the touchstone's side—
But rain and thunder not, lest they be terrified.

XXXVIII

On some rich balcony where sleep the doves,
Through the dark night with thy belovèd stay,
The lightning weary with the sport she loves;
But with the sunrise journey on thy way—
For they that labour for a friend do not delay.

XXXIX

The gallant dries his mistress' tears that stream
When he returns at dawn to her embrace—
Prevent thou not the sun's bright-fingered beam
That wipes the tear-dew from the lotus' face;
His anger else were great, and great were thy disgrace.

XL

the cloud is besought to travel to Deep River.

Thy winsome shadow-soul will surely find
An entrance in Deep River's current bright,
As thoughts find entrance in a placid mind;
Then let no rudeness of thine own affright
The darting fish that seem her glances lotus-white.

XLI

But steal her sombre veil of mist away,
Although her reeds seem hands that clutch the dress
To hide her charms; thou hast no time to stay,
Yet who that once has known a dear caress
Could bear to leave a woman's unveiled loveliness?

XLII

Thence to Holy Peak,

The breeze 'neath which the breathing acre grants
New odours, and the forest figs hang sleek,
With pleasant whistlings drunk by elephants
Through long and hollow trunks, will gently seek
To waft thee onward fragrantly to Holy Peak.

XLIII

the dwelling-place of Skanda, god of war, the child of Shiva and Gauri, concerning whose birth more than one quaint tale is told.

There change thy form; become a cloud of flowers
With heavenly moisture wet, and pay the meed
Of praise to Skanda with thy blossom showers;
That sun-outshining god is Shiva's seed,
Fire-born to save the heavenly hosts in direst need.

XLIV

God Skanda's peacock—he whose eyeballs shine
By Shiva's moon, whose flashing fallen plume
The god's fond mother wears, a gleaming line
Over her ear beside the lotus bloom—
Will dance to thunders echoing in the caverns' room.

XLV

Thence to Skin River, so called because it flowed forth from a mountain of cattle carcasses, offered in sacrifice by the pious emperor Rantideva.

Adore the reed-born god and speed away,
While Siddhas flee, lest rain should put to shame
The lutes which they devoutly love to play;
But pause to glorify the stream whose name
Recalls the sacrificing emperor's blessèd fame.

XLVI

Narrow the river seems from heaven's blue;
And gods above, who see her dainty line
Matched, when thou drinkest, with thy darker hue,
Will think they see a pearly necklace twine
Round Earth, with one great sapphire in its midst ashine.

XLVII

The province of the Ten Cities.

Beyond, the province of Ten Cities lies
Whose women, charming with their glances rash,
Will view thine image with bright, eager eyes,
Dark eyes that dance beneath the lifted lash,
As when black bees round nodding jasmine-blossoms flash.

XLVIII

The Hallowed Land, where were fought the awful battles of the ancient epic time.

Then veil the Hallowed Land in cloudy shade;
Visit the field where to this very hour
Lie bones that sank beneath the soldier's blade,
Where Arjuna discharged his arrowy shower
On men, as thou thy rain-jets on the lotus-flower.

XLIX

In these battles, the hero Balarama, whose weapon was a plough-share, would take no part, because kinsmen of his were fighting in each army. He preferred to spend the time in drinking from the holy river Sarasvati, though little accustomed to any other drink than wine.

Sweet friend, drink where those holy waters shine
Which the plough-bearing hero—loath to fight

His kinsmen—rather drank than sweetest wine
With a loving bride's reflected eyes alight;
Then, though thy form be black, thine inner soul is bright.

L

The Ganges River, which originates in heaven. Its fall is broken by the head of Shiva, who stands on the Himalaya Mountains; otherwise the shock would be too great for the earth. But Shiva's goddess-bride is displeased.

Fly then where Ganges o'er the king of mountains
Falls like a flight of stairs from heaven let down
For the sons of men; she hurls her billowy fountains
Like hands to grasp the moon on Shiva's crown
And laughs her foamy laugh at Gauri's jealous frown.

LI

The dark cloud is permitted to mingle with the clear stream of Ganges, as the muddy Jumna River does near the city now called Allahabad.

If thou, like some great elephant of the sky,
Shouldst wish from heaven's eminence to bend
And taste the crystal stream, her beauties high—
As thy dark shadows with her whiteness blend—
Would be what Jumna's waters at Prayaga lend.

LII

The magnificent Himalaya range.

Her birth-place is Himalaya's rocky crest
Whereon the scent of musk is never lost,
For deer rest ever there where thou wilt rest
Sombre against the peak with whiteness glossed,
Like dark earth by the snow-white bull of Shiva tossed.

LIII

If, born from friction of the deodars,
A scudding fire should prove the mountain's bane,
Singeing the tails of yaks with fiery stars,
Quench thou the flame with countless streams of rain—
The great have power that they may soothe distress and pain.

LIV

If mountain monsters should assail thy path
With angry leaps that of their object fail,
Only to hurt themselves in helpless wrath,
Scatter the creatures with thy pelting hail—
For who is not despised that strives without avail?

LV

Bend lowly down and move in reverent state
Round Shiva's foot-print on the rocky plate
With offerings laden by the saintly great;
The sight means heaven as their eternal fate
When death and sin are past, for them that faithful wait.

LVI

The breeze is piping on the bamboo-tree;
And choirs of heaven sing in union sweet
O'er demon foe of Shiva's victory;
If thunders in the caverns drumlike beat,
Then surely Shiva's symphony will be complete.

LVII

The mountain pass called the Swan-gate.

Pass by the wonders of the snowy slope;
Through the Swan-gate, through mountain masses rent
To make his fame a path by Bhrigu's hope
In long, dark beauty fly, still northward bent,
Like Vishnu's foot, when he sought the demon's chastisement.

LVIII

And at Mount Kailasa, the long journey is ended;

Seek then Kailasa's hospitable care,
With peaks by magic arms asunder riven,
To whom, as mirror, goddesses repair,
So lotus-bright his summits cloud the heaven,
Like form and substance to God's daily laughter given.

LIX

Like powder black and soft I seem to see
Thine outline on the mountain slope as bright
As new-sawn tusks of stainless ivory;
No eye could wink before as fair a sight
As dark-blue robes upon the Ploughman's shoulder white.

LX

Should Shiva throw his serpent-ring aside
And give Gauri his hand, go thou before
Upon the mount of joy to be their guide;
Conceal within thee all thy watery store
And seem a terraced stairway to the jewelled floor.

LXI

I doubt not that celestial maidens sweet
With pointed bracelet gems will prick thee there
To make of thee a shower-bath in the heat;
Frighten the playful girls if they should dare
To keep thee longer, friend, with thunder's harshest blare.

LXII

Drink where the golden lotus dots the lake;
Serve Indra's elephant as a veil to hide
His drinking; then the tree of wishing shake,
Whose branches like silk garments flutter wide:
With sports like these, O cloud, enjoy the mountain side.

LXIII

for on this mountain is the city of the Yakshas.

Then, in familiar Alaka find rest,
Down whom the Ganges' silken river swirls,
Whose towers cling to her mountain lover's breast,
While clouds adorn her face like glossy curls
And streams of rain like strings of close-inwoven pearls.

LATTER CLOUD

I

The splendid heavenly city Alaka,

Where palaces in much may rival thee—
Their ladies gay, thy lightning's dazzling powers—
Symphonic drums, thy thunder's melody—
Their bright mosaic floors, thy silver showers—
Thy rainbow, paintings, and thy height, cloud-licking towers.

II

where the flowers which on earth blossom at different seasons, are all found in bloom the year round.

Where the autumn lotus in dear fingers shines,
And lodh-flowers' April dust on faces rare,
Spring amaranth with winter jasmine twines
In women's braids, and summer siris fair,
The rainy madder in the parting of their hair.

III

Here grows the magic tree which yields whatever is desired.

Where men with maids whose charm no blemish mars
Climb to the open crystal balcony
Inlaid with flower-like sparkling of the stars,
And drink the love-wine from the wishing-tree,
And listen to the drums' deep-thundering dignity.

IV

Where maidens whom the gods would gladly wed
Are fanned by breezes cool with Ganges' spray
In shadows that the trees of heaven spread;
In golden sands at hunt-the-pearl they play,
Bury their little fists, and draw them void away.

V

Where lovers' passion-trembling fingers cling
To silken robes whose sashes flutter wide,
The knots undone; and red-lipped women fling,
Silly with shame, their rouge from side to side,
Hoping in vain the flash of jewelled lamps to hide.

VI

Where, brought to balconies' palatial tops
By ever-blowing guides, were clouds before
Like thee who spotted paintings with their drops;
Then, touched with guilty fear, were seen no more,
But scattered smoke-like through the lattice' grated door.

VII

Here are the stones from which drops of water ooze when the moon shines on them.

Where from the moonstones hung in nets of thread
Great drops of water trickle in the night—
When the moon shines clear and thou, O cloud, art fled—
To ease the languors of the women's plight
Who lie relaxed and tired in love's embraces tight.

VIII

Here are the magic gardens of heaven.

Where lovers, rich with hidden wealth untold,
Wander each day with nymphs for ever young,
Enjoy the wonders that the gardens hold,
The Shining Gardens, where the praise is sung
Of the god of wealth by choirs with love-impassioned tongue.

IX

Where sweet nocturnal journeys are betrayed
At sunrise by the fallen flowers from curls
That fluttered as they stole along afraid,
By leaves, by golden lotuses, by pearls,
By broken necklaces that slipped from winsome girls.

X

Here the god of love is not seen, because of the presence of his great enemy, Shiva. Yet his absence is not severely felt.

Where the god of love neglects his bee-strung bow,
Since Shiva's friendship decks Kubera's reign;
His task is done by clever maids, for lo!
Their frowning missile glances, darting plain
At lover-targets, never pass the mark in vain.

XI

Here the goddesses have all needful ornaments. For the Mine of Sentiment declares: "Women everywhere have four kinds of ornaments—hair-ornaments, jewels, clothes, cosmetics; anything else is local."

Where the wishing-tree yields all that might enhance
The loveliness of maidens young and sweet:
Bright garments, wine that teaches eyes to dance,
And flowering twigs, and rarest gems discrete,
And lac-dye fit to stain their pretty lotus-feet.

XII

And here is the home of the unhappy Yaksha,

There, northward from the master's palace, see
Our home, whose rainbow-gateway shines afar;
And near it grows a little coral-tree,
Bending 'neath many a blossom's clustered star,
Loved by my bride as children of adoption are.

XIII

with its artificial pool;

A pool is near, to which an emerald stair
Leads down, with blooming lotuses of gold
Whose stalks are polished beryl; resting there,
The wistful swans are glad when they behold
Thine image, and forget the lake they loved of old.

XIV

its hill of sport, girdled by bright hedges, like the dark cloud girdled by the lightning;

And on the bank, a sapphire-crested hill
Round which the golden plantain-hedges fit;

She loves the spot; and while I marvel still
At thee, my friend, as flashing lightnings flit
About thine edge, with restless rapture I remember it.

XV

its two favourite trees, which will not blossom while their mistress is grieving;

The ashoka-tree, with sweetly dancing lines,
The favourite bakul-tree, are near the bower
Of amaranth-engirdled jasmine-vines;
Like me, they wait to feel the winning power
Of her persuasion, ere they blossom into flower.

XVI

its tame peacock;

A golden pole is set between the pair,
With crystal perch above its emerald bands
As green as young bamboo; at sunset there
Thy friend, the blue-necked peacock, rises, stands,
And dances when she claps her bracelet-tinkling hands.

XVII

and its painted emblems of the god of wealth.

These are the signs—recall them o'er and o'er,
My clever friend—by which the house is known,
And the Conch and Lotus painted by the door:
Alas! when I am far, the charm is gone—
The lotus' loveliness is lost with set of sun.

XVIII

Small as the elephant cub thou must become
For easy entrance; rest where gems enhance
The glory of the hill beside my home,
And peep into the house with lightning-glance,
But make its brightness dim as fireflies' twinkling dance.

XIX

The Yaksha's bride.

The supremest woman from God's workshop gone—
Young, slender; little teeth and red, red lips,
Slight waist and gentle eyes of timid fawn,
An idly graceful movement, generous hips,
Fair bosom into which the sloping shoulder slips—

XX

Like a bird that mourns her absent mate anew
Passing these heavy days in longings keen,
My girlish wife whose words are sweet and few,
My second life, shall there of thee be seen—
But changed like winter-blighted lotus-blooms, I ween.

XXI

Her eyes are swol'n with tears that stream unchidden;
Her lips turn pale with sorrow's burning sighs;
The face that rests upon her hand is hidden
By hanging curls, as when the glory dies
Of the suffering moon pursued by thee through nightly skies.

XXII

The passion of love passes through ten stages, eight of which are suggested in this stanza and the stanzas which follow. The first stage is not indicated; it is called Exchange of Glances.

Thou first wilt see her when she seeks relief
In worship; or, half fancying, half recalling,
She draws mine image worn by absent grief;
Or asks the cagèd, sweetly-singing starling:
"Do you remember, dear, our lord? You were his darling."

XXIII

In this stanza and the preceding one is suggested the second stage: Wistfulness.

Or holds a lute on her neglected skirt,
And tries to sing of me, and tries in vain;
For she dries the tear-wet string with hands inert,
And e'er begins, and e'er forgets again,
Though she herself composed it once, the loving strain.

XXIV

Here is suggested the third stage: Desire.

Or counts the months of absence yet remaining
With flowers laid near the threshold on the floor,
Or tastes the bliss of hours when love was gaining
The memories recollected o'er and o'er—
A woman's comforts when her lonely heart is sore.

XXV

Here is suggested the fourth stage: Wakefulness.

Such daytime labours doubtless ease the ache
Which doubly hurts her in the helpless dark;
With news from me a keener joy to wake,
Stand by her window in the night, and mark
My sleepless darling on her pallet hard and stark.

XXVI

Here is suggested the fifth stage: Emaciation.

Resting one side upon that widowed bed,
Like the slender moon upon the Eastern height,
So slender she, now worn with anguish dread,
Passing with stifling tears the long, sad night
Which, spent in love with me, seemed but a moment's flight.

XXVII

Here is suggested the sixth stage: Loss of Interest in Ordinary Pleasures.

On the cool, sweet moon that through the lattice flashes
She looks with the old delight, then turns away
And veils her eyes with water-weighted lashes,
Sad as the flower that blooms in sunlight gay,
But cannot wake nor slumber on a cloudy day.

XXVIII

Here is suggested the seventh stage: Loss of Youthful Bashfulness.

One unanointed curl still frets her cheek
When tossed by sighs that burn her blossom-lip;
And still she yearns, and still her yearnings seek
That we might be united though in sleep—
Ah! Happy dreams come not to brides that ever weep.

XXIX

Here is suggested the eighth stage: Absent-mindedness. For if she were not absent-minded, she would arrange the braid so as not to be annoyed by it.

Her single tight-bound braid she pushes oft—
With a hand uncared for in her lonely madness—
So rough it seems, from the cheek that is so soft:
That braid ungarlanded since the first day's sadness,
Which I shall loose again when troubles end in gladness.

XXX

Here is suggested the ninth stage: Prostration.
The tenth stage, Death, is not suggested.

The delicate body, weak and suffering,
Quite unadorned and tossing to and fro
In oft-renewing wretchedness, will wring
Even from thee a raindrop-tear, I know—
Soft breasts like thine are pitiful to others' woe.

XXXI

I know her bosom full of love for me,
And therefore fancy how her soul doth grieve
In this our first divorce; it cannot be
Self-flattery that idle boastings weave—
Soon shalt thou see it all, and seeing, shalt believe.

XXXII

Quivering of the eyelids

Her hanging hair prevents the twinkling shine
Of fawn-eyes that forget their glances sly,
Lost to the friendly aid of rouge and wine—
Yet the eyelids quiver when thou drawest nigh
As water-lilies do when fish go scurrying by.

XXXIII

and trembling of the limbs are omens of
speedy union with the beloved.

And limbs that thrill to thee thy welcome prove,
Limbs fair as stems in some rich plantain-bower,
No longer showing marks of my rough love,
Robbed of their cooling pearls by fatal power,
The limbs which I was wont to soothe in passion's hour.

XXXIV

But if she should be lost in happy sleep,
Wait, bear with her, grant her but three hours' grace,
And thunder not, O cloud, but let her keep
The dreaming vision of her lover's face—
Loose not too soon the imagined knot of that embrace.

XXXV

As thou wouldst wake the jasmine's budding wonder,
Wake her with breezes blowing mistily;
Conceal thy lightnings, and with words of thunder
Speak boldly, though she answer haughtily
With eyes that fasten on the lattice and on thee.

XXXVI

The cloud is instructed how to announce himself

"Thou art no widow; for thy husband's friend
Is come to tell thee what himself did say—
A cloud with low, sweet thunder-tones that send
All weary wanderers hastening on their way,
Eager to loose the braids of wives that lonely stay."

XXXVII

in such a way as to win the favour of his auditor.

Say this, and she will welcome thee indeed,
Sweet friend, with a yearning heart's tumultuous beating
And joy-uplifted eyes; and she will heed
The after message: such a friendly greeting
Is hardly less to woman's heart than lovers' meeting.

XXXVIII

The message itself.

Thus too, my king, I pray of thee to speak,
Remembering kindness is its own reward;
"Thy lover lives, and from the holy peak
Asks if these absent days good health afford—
Those born to pain must ever use this opening word.

XXXIX

With body worn as thine, with pain as deep,
With tears and ceaseless longings answering thine,
With sighs more burning than the sighs that keep
Thy lips ascorch—doomed far from thee to pine,
He too doth weave the fancies that thy soul entwine.

XL

He used to love, when women friends were near,
To whisper things he might have said aloud
That he might touch thy face and kiss thine ear;
Unheard and even unseen, no longer proud,
He now must send this yearning message by a cloud.

XLI

According to the treatise called "Virtue's Banner," a lover has four solaces in separation: first, looking at objects that remind him of her he loves;

'I see thy limbs in graceful-creeping vines,
Thy glances in the eyes of gentle deer,
Thine eyebrows in the ripple's dancing lines,
Thy locks in plumes, thy face in moonlight clear—
Ah, jealous! But the whole sweet image is not here.

XLII

second, painting a picture of her;

And when I paint that loving jealousy
With chalk upon the rock, and my caress
As at thy feet I lie, I cannot see
Through tears that to mine eyes unbidden press—
So stern a fate denies a painted happiness.

XLIII

third, dreaming of her;

And when I toss mine arms to clasp thee tight,
Mine own though but in visions of a dream—
They who behold the oft-repeated sight,
The kind divinities of wood and stream,
Let fall great pearly tears that on the blossoms gleam.

XLIV

fourth, touching something which she has touched.

Himalaya's breeze blows gently from the north,
Unsheathing twigs upon the deodar
And sweet with sap that it entices forth—
I embrace it lovingly; it came so far,
Perhaps it touched thee first, my life's unchanging star!

XLV

Oh, might the long, long night seem short to me!
Oh, might the day his hourly tortures hide!
Such longings for the things that cannot be,
Consume my helpless heart, sweet-glancing bride,
In burning agonies of absence from thy side.

XLVI

The bride is besought not to lose heart at hearing of her lover's wretchedness,

Yet much reflection, dearest, makes me strong,
Strong with an inner strength; nor shouldst thou feel
Despair at what has come to us of wrong;
Who has unending woe or lasting weal?
Our fates move up and down upon a circling wheel.

XLVII

and to remember that the curse has its appointed end, when the rainy season is over and the year of exile fulfilled. Vishnu spends the rainy months in sleep upon the back of the cosmic serpent Shesha.

When Vishnu rises from his serpent bed
The curse is ended; close thine eyelids tight
And wait till only four months more are sped;
Then we shall taste each long-desired delight
Through nights that the full autumn moon illumines bright.

XLVIII

Then is added a secret which, as it could not possibly be known to a third person, assures her that the cloud is a true messenger.

And one thing more: thou layest once asleep,
Clasping my neck, then wakening with a scream;
And when I wondered why, thou couldst but weep
A while, and then a smile began to beam:
"Rogue! Rogue! I saw thee with another girl in dream."

XLIX

This memory shows me cheerful, gentle wife;
Then let no gossip thy suspicions move:
They say the affections strangely forfeit life
In separation, but in truth they prove
Toward the absent dear, a growing bulk of tenderest love.' "

L

The Yaksha then begs the cloud to return with a message of comfort,

Console her patient heart, to breaking full
In our first separation; having spoken,
Fly from the mountain ploughed by Shiva's bull;
Make strong with message and with tender token
My life, so easily, like morning jasmines, broken.

LI

I hope, sweet friend, thou grantest all my suit,
Nor read refusal in thy solemn air;
When thirsty birds complain, thou givest mute
The rain from heaven: such simple hearts are rare,
Whose only answer is fulfilment of the prayer.

LII

and dismisses him, with a prayer for his welfare.

Thus, though I pray unworthy, answer me
For friendship's sake, or pity's, magnified
By the sight of my distress; then wander free
In rainy loveliness, and ne'er abide
One moment's separation from thy lightning bride.

THE SEASONS

THE SEASONS

The Seasons is an unpretentious poem, describing in six short cantos the six seasons into which the Hindus divide the year. The title is perhaps a little misleading, as the description is not objective, but deals with the feelings awakened by each season in a pair of young lovers. Indeed, the poem might be called a Lover's Calendar. Kalidasa's authorship has been doubted, without very cogent argument. The question is not of much interest, as *The Seasons* would neither add greatly to his reputation nor subtract from it.

The whole poem contains one hundred and forty-four stanzas, or something less than six hundred lines of verse. There follow a few stanzas selected from each canto.

Summer

Pitiless heat from heaven pours
By day, but nights are cool;
Continual bathing gently lowers
The water in the pool;
The evening brings a charming peace:
For summer-time is here
When love that never knows surcease,
Is less imperious, dear.

Yet love can never fall asleep;
For he is waked to-day
By songs that all their sweetness keep
And lutes that softly play,
By fans with sandal-water wet
That bring us drowsy rest,
By strings of pearls that gently fret
Full many a lovely breast.

The sunbeams like the fires are hot
That on the altar wake;

The enmity is quite forgot
  Of peacock and of snake;
The peacock spares his ancient foe,
  For pluck and hunger fail;
He hides his burning head below
  The shadow of his tail.

Beneath the garland of the rays
  That leave no corner cool,
The water vanishes in haze
  And leaves a muddy pool;
The cobra does not hunt for food
  Nor heed the frog at all
Who finds beneath the serpent's hood
  A sheltering parasol.

Dear maiden of the graceful song,
  To you may summer's power
Bring moonbeams clear and garlands long
  And breath of trumpet-flower,
Bring lakes that countless lilies dot,
  Refreshing water-sprays,
Sweet friends at evening, and a spot
  Cool after burning days.

The Rains

The rain advances like a king
  In awful majesty;
Hear, dearest, how his thunders ring
  Like royal drums, and see
His lightning-banners wave; a cloud
  For elephant he rides,
And finds his welcome from the crowd
  Of lovers and of brides.

The clouds, a mighty army, march
  With drumlike thundering
And stretch upon the rainbow's arch
  The lightning's flashing string;

The cruel arrows of the rain
  Smite them who love, apart
From whom they love, with stinging pain,
  And pierce them to the heart.

The forest seems to show its glee
  In flowering nipa plants;
In waving twigs of many a tree
  Wind-swept, it seems to dance;
Its ketak-blossom's opening sheath
  Is like a smile put on
To greet the rain's reviving breath,
  Now pain and heat are gone.

To you, dear, may the cloudy time
  Bring all that you desire,
Bring every pleasure, perfect, prime,
  To set a bride on fire;
May rain whereby life wakes and shines
  Where there is power of life,
The unchanging friend of clinging vines,
  Shower blessings on my wife.

Autumn

The autumn comes, a maiden fair
  In slenderness and grace,
With nodding rice-stems in her hair
  And lilies in her face.
In flowers of grasses she is clad;
  And as she moves along,
Birds greet her with their cooing glad
  Like bracelets' tinkling song.

A diadem adorns the night
  Of multitudinous stars;
Her silken robe is white moonlight,
  Set free from cloudy bars;
And on her face (the radiant moon)
  Bewitching smiles are shown:

She seems a slender maid, who soon
  Will be a woman grown.

Over the rice-fields, laden plants
  Are shivering to the breeze;
While in his brisk caresses dance
  The blossom-burdened trees;
He ruffles every lily-pond
  Where blossoms kiss and part,
And stirs with lover's fancies fond
  The young man's eager heart.

Winter

The bloom of tenderer flowers is past
  And lilies droop forlorn,
For winter-time is come at last,
  Rich with its ripened corn;
Yet for the wealth of blossoms lost
  Some hardier flowers appear
That bid defiance to the frost
  Of sterner days, my dear.

The vines, remembering summer, shiver
  In frosty winds, and gain
A fuller life from mere endeavour
  To live through all that pain;
Yet in the struggle and acquist
  They turn as pale and wan
As lonely women who have missed
  Known love, now lost and gone.

Then may these winter days show forth
  To you each known delight,
Bring all that women count as worth
  Pure happiness and bright;
While villages, with bustling cry,
  Bring home the ripened corn,
And herons wheel through wintry sky,
  Forget sad thoughts forlorn.

Early Spring

Now, dearest, lend a heedful ear
  And listen while I sing
Delights to every maiden dear,
  The charms of early spring:
When earth is dotted with the heaps
  Of corn, when heron-scream
Is rare but sweet, when passion leaps
  And paints a livelier dream.

When all must cheerfully applaud
  A blazing open fire;
Or if they needs must go abroad,
  The sun is their desire;
When everybody hopes to find
  The frosty chill allayed
By garments warm, a window-blind
  Shut, and a sweet young maid.

Then may the days of early spring
  For you be rich and full
With love's proud, soft philandering
  And many a candy-pull,
With sweetest rice and sugar-cane:
  And may you float above
The absent grieving and the pain
  Of separated love.

Spring

A stalwart soldier comes, the spring,
  Who bears the bow of Love;
And on that bow, the lustrous string
  Is made of bees, that move
With malice as they speed the shaft
  Of blossoming mango-flower
At us, dear, who have never laughed
  At love, nor scorned his power.

Their blossom-burden weights the trees;
  The winds in fragrance move;
The lakes are bright with lotuses,
  The women bright with love;
The days are soft, the evenings clear
  And charming; everything
That moves and lives and blossoms, dear,
  Is sweeter in the spring.

The groves are beautifully bright
  For many and many a mile
With jasmine-flowers that are as white
  As loving woman's smile:
The resolution of a saint
  Might well be tried by this;
Far more, young hearts that fancies paint
  With dreams of loving bliss.